The New Native American Novel

WORKS IN PROGRESS

N. Scott Momaday, *Elder*. Pen and ink on Arches paper, 24 by 30 inches

The New Native American Novel

WORKS IN PROGRESS

Edited by
Mary Dougherty Bartlett

Published for New America
by the University of New Mexico Press
Albuquerque

Library of Congress Cataloging-in-Publication Data
Main entry under title:

The New native American novel.

　1. American fiction—Indian authors. 2. American
fiction—20th century. 3. Indians of North America—
Fiction. I. Bartlett, Mary Dougherty.
PS508.I5N49 1986　　813.54080897　　85-16565
ISBN 0–8263–0849–X
ISBN 0–8263–0853–8

This issue of *New America* has been funded in part by The New Mexico Arts Division, National Endowment for the Arts, The Coordinating Council of Literary Magazines, The University of New Mexico, and the Graduate Student Association of the University of New Mexico.

Design: B. Jellow

Contents

Preface

Novels by American Indian writers have been a part of American literature since 1899, when Simon Pokagon published his *O-Gî-Mäw-Kwe Mit-I-Gwä-Kî, Queen of the Woods,* or even longer if we claim John Rollin Ridge's *The Life and Adventures of Joaquin Murieta* as novel rather than biography as some critics have insisted upon doing. Following Pokagon, American Indian writers such as D'Arcy McNickle, John Joseph Mathews, John Milton Oskison, and Hum-Ishu-Ma (Mourning Dove) kept a steady, though slight, stream of novels appearing through the twenties and thirties. It wasn't until 1969, however, when N. Scott Momaday won a Pulitzer Prize for his first, extraordinary novel, *House Made of Dawn,* that the stream of novels by Indian writers became a flood, with novels appearing in quick succession by Janet Campbell Hale, Nasnaga

(Roger Russell), Chief George Pierre, Dallas Chief Eagle, Denton R. Bedford, James Welch, Hyemeyohsts Storm, Virginia Driving Hawk Sneve, Gerald Vizenor, and Leslie Silko. In 1979 D'Arcy McNickle's third novel, *Wind From An Enemy Sky,* appeared posthumously, and since that time Paula Gunn Allen, Louise Erdrich, and Janet Campbell Hale have added impressively to the growing list of novels by Indian women.

In this collection, we have attempted to bring together excerpts from current works-in-progress by both published and unpublished novelists in a desire to suggest what the future may hold. Perhaps the most familiar name here will be that of Scott Momaday, whose *House Made of Dawn* must be considered a seminal work for all Indian writers. Other previously published novelists included here are Gerald Vizenor, whose *Darkness in Saint Louis Bearheart* (1978) underscored a radical and exciting departure in American Indian fiction, and Paula Gunn Allen, whose *The Woman Who Owned the Shadows* (1983) announced the re-emergence of the voice of the Indian woman in the novel. Finally, in the excerpt from Louise Erdrich's forthcoming novel, *The Beet Queen,* we have in this collection a work from one of the most exciting of contemporary American novelists, whose first novel, *Love Medicine,* received the prestigious 1984 National Book Critics Circle Award.

Previously unpublished novelists appearing here with excerpts from works-in-progress include writers better known for their work in poetry, short fiction, and criticism or other nonfiction areas, writers such as Linda Hogan, Elizabeth Cook-Lynn, Glen Martin, and Louis Owens, each of whom has published in numerous magazines, journals, or anthologies.

We are grateful not only to those who contributed parts of novels for this volume, but also to Sam English and writer-painter N. Scott Momaday for providing us with artwork and to Elizabeth Hadas and the UNM Press for their support and invaluable assistance in making this publication possible.

The New Native American Novel

The Manifestation at Argus

from *The Beet Queen*
Louise Erdrich

Sita Kozka

My cousin Mary came in on the early freight train one morning, with nothing but an old blue keepsake box full of worthless pins and buttons. My father picked her up in his arms and carried her down the hallway into the kitchen. I was too old to be carried. He sat her down, then my mother said, "Go clean the counters, Sita." So I don't know what lies she told them after that.

Later on that morning, my parents put her to sleep in my bed. When I objected to this, saying that she could sleep on the trundle, my mother said, "Cry sakes, you can sleep there too, you know." And that is how I ended up that night, crammed in the trundle, which is too short for me. I slept with my legs dangling out in the cold air. I didn't feel welcoming toward Mary the next morning, and who can blame me?

[3]

Besides, on her first waking day in Argus, there were the clothes.

It is a good thing she opened the blue keepsake box at breakfast and found little bits of trash, like I said, because if I had not felt sorry for my cousin that day, I would not have stood for Mary and my mother ripping through my closet and bureau. "This fits perfectly," my mother said, holding up one of my favorite blouses, "try it on!" And Mary did. Then she put it in her drawer, which was another thing. I had to clear out two of my bureau drawers for her.

"Mother," I said, after this had gone on for some time and I was beginning to think I would have to wear the same three outfits all the next school year, "Mother, this has really gone far enough."

"Crap," said my mother, who talks that way, "your cousin hasn't got a stitch."

Yet she had half of mine by then, quite a wardrobe, and all the time it was increasing as my mother got more excited about dressing the poor orphan. But Mary wasn't really an orphan, although she played on that for sympathy. Her mother was still alive even if she had left my cousin, which I doubted. I really thought that Mary just ran away from her mother because she could not appreciate Adelaide's style. It's not everyone who understands how to use their good looks to the best advantage. My Aunt Adelaide did. She was always my favorite, and I just died for her to visit. But she didn't come often because my mother couldn't understand style either.

"Who are you trying to impress?" she'd hoot when Adelaide came out to dinner in a dress with a fur collar. My father would blush red and cut his meat. He didn't say much, but I knew he did not approve of Adelaide any more than her older sister did. My mother said she'd always spoiled Adelaide because she was the baby of the family. She said the same of me. But I don't think that I was ever spoiled, not one iota, because I had to work the same as anyone cleaning gizzards.

I hated Wednesdays because that was the day we killed chickens. The farmer brought them stacked in cages made of thin wooden slats. One by one, Canute, who did most of the slaughtering, killed them by sticking their necks with the blade of his long knife. After the chickens were killed, plucked, and cut open, I got the gizzards. Coffee can after coffee can full of gizzards. I still have dreams. I had to turn each gizzard inside out and wash it in a pan of water. All the gravel and hard seed fell out into the bottom. Sometimes I found bits of metal and broken glass. Once I found a brilliant. "Mother!" I yelled, holding it out in my palm, "I found a diamond!" Everyone was so excited that they clustered around me. And then my mother took the little sparkling stone to the window. It didn't scratch the glass at all, of course, and I had to clean the rest of the gizzards. But for a moment I was sure that the diamond had made us rich, which brings me to another diamond. A cow's diamond, my inheritance.

It was a joke, really, about the inheritance, at least it was a joke to my Papa. A cow's diamond is the hard, rounded lens inside a cow's eye that shines when you look through it at the light, almost like an opal. You could never make a ring of it or use it for any kind of jewelry, since it might shatter, and of course it had no worth. My father mainly carried it as a lucky piece. He'd flip it in the air between customers and sometimes in a game of cribbage I'd see him rub it. I wanted it. One day I asked if he would give it to me.

"I can't," he said. "It's my butcher's luck. It can be your inheritance, how about that?"

I suppose my mouth dropped open in surprise because my father always gave me anything I asked for. For instance, we had a small glass candy case out front, over the sausages, and I could eat candy any time I wanted. I used to bring rootbeer barrels into class for the girls I liked. I never chewed gumballs, though, because I heard Auntie Adelaide tell mother once, in anger, that only tramps chewed gum. This was when my mother was trying to quit smoking and she kept a sack of gumballs in the pocket of her apron. I was in the kitchen with them when they had this argument. "Tramps!" my mother said, "That's the pot calling the kettle black!" Then she took the gum from her mouth and rubbed it into Adelaide's long wavy hair. "I'll kill you!" my Auntie raged. It was something to see grown-ups behaving this way, but I don't blame Auntie Adelaide. I'd feel the same if I had to cut a big knot of gum out like she did, and have a short patch of hair. I never chewed gum. But anything else in the store I wanted, I just took. Or I asked and it was handed right over. So you can see why my father's refusal was a surprise. The cow's diamond was the first thing I asked for that he never gave.

I had my pride even as a child, and I never mentioned it again. But here is what happened two days after Mary Lavelle came.

We were waiting to be tucked in that night. I was in my own bed, and she was in the trundle. She was short enough to fit there without hanging off the edge. The last thing she did before going to sleep was put Adelaide's old keepsake box up on my bureau. I didn't say anything, but really it was sad. I guess my Papa thought so too. I guess he took pity on her. That night he came in the room, he tucked the blankets around me, kissed me on the forehead, and said "Sleep tight." Then he bent over Mary and kissed her too. But to Mary he said, "Here is a jewel."

It was the cow's diamond that I wanted, the butcher's luck. When I looked over the edge of my bed and saw the pale lens glowing in her hand, I could have spit. I pretended to be asleep when she asked me what it was. Find out for yourself, I thought, and said nothing. A few weeks later, when she knew her way around town, she got some jeweler to drill a hole through one end of the lucky piece. Then she hung the cow's diamond around her neck on a piece of string, as if it were something valuable. Later on she got a gold-link chain.

First my room, then my clothing, then the cow's diamond. But the worst was yet to come when she stole Celestine.

My best friend Celestine lived three miles out of town with her half-brother and much older half-sisters, who were Indians. There weren't all that many who came down from the reservation, but Celestine's mother had been one. She worked for Dutch James, keeping his house when he was a bachelor, and after, once they married and Celestine was born. I overheard where Celestine came just a month past the wedding, in fact, just before her mother brought down the three other children Dutch James hadn't known about. Somehow, as it worked out, they all lived together up until the time of Dutch James' peculiar death. He froze solid in our very meat locker. But that is an event no one in this house will discuss.

Anyway, those others were never court adopted and went by the last name Kashpaw. Celestine was a James. Because her mother died when Celestine was young, it was the influence of Dutch James that was more important to Celestine. He'd known the French language, and sometimes she spoke French to lord it over us in school, but more often she got teased for her size, and the odd flimsy clothes that her sisters picked out of the dimestore in Argus.

Celestine was tall, but not clumsy. More what my mother called statuesque. Nobody told Celestine what to do. We came and went and played anywhere we felt like. My mother would never have let me play in a graveyard, for example, but when visiting Celestine that's what we did. There was a cemetery right on the land of Dutch James' homestead, a place filled with the graves of children who died in some plague of cough or flu. They'd been forgotten, except by us. Their little crosses of wood or bent iron were tilted. We had to straighten them, even recarve the names with a kitchen knife. We dug up violets from the oxbow and weeded around the splintered markers. The graveyard was our place, because of what we did, and we liked to sit there on a hot afternoon, it was so pleasant. Wind ruffled the long grass, worms sifted the earth below us, swallows from the mud banks dove through the sky in pairs. It was a nice place, really, not even very sad. But of course Mary had to ruin it.

I underestimated Mary Lavelle. Or perhaps I was too trusting, since it was I who suggested we go visit Celestine one day in early summer. I started out by giving Mary a ride on the handlebars of my bicycle, but she was so heavy I could hardly steer.

"You pedal," I said, stopping in the road. She fell off, then jumped up and stood the bicycle upright. I suppose I was heavy, too. But her legs were tireless. Celestine's Indian half-brother, Russell, approached us on the way to Celestine's. "Who's your slave today?" he said. "She's cuter than you'll ever be!" I knew he said things like that because he meant the opposite, but Mary didn't. I felt her swell proudly in my old blue plaid dress. She made it all the way to Celestine's and when we got there I jumped off and ran straight in the door.

Celestine was baking, just like a grown-up. She could make anything she wanted, no matter how sweet. Celestine and Mary mixed up a batch of cookie dough. Mary liked cooking, too. I didn't. So they measured and stirred, timed the stove, and put out the cooling racks while I sat at the table with a piece of waxed paper, rolled out the dough, and cut it into fancy shapes.

"Where did you come from?" Celestine asked Mary as we worked.

"She came from Hollywood," I said. Celestine laughed at that, but then she saw it wasn't funny to Mary, and she stopped.

"Truly," said Celestine.

"Minnesota," said Mary.

"Are your mother and father still there?" asked Celestine. "Are they still alive?"

"They're dead," said Mary promptly. My mouth fell open before I could get a word of truth in.

"Mine are dead too," Celestine said.

And then I knew why Celestine had been asking these questions, when she already knew the whole story and its details from me. Mary and Celestine smiled into each other's eyes, I could see that it was like two people meeting in a crowd, who knew each other from a long time before. And what was also odd, they suddenly looked alike. It was only when they were together. You'd never notice it when they weren't. Celestine's hair was a tarnished red brown, her skin was olive, her eyes burning black. Mary's eyes were bright brown and her hair was dark and lank. Together, like I said, they looked similar. It wasn't even their build. Mary was short and stocky, while Celestine was tall. It was something else, either in the way they acted or the way they talked. Maybe it was a common sort of fierceness that orphans have.

After they went back to their mixing and measuring, I could see that they were friendlier, too. They stood close together, touched shoulders, laughed and admired everything the other one did until it made me sick.

"Mary's going to Saint Catherine's next fall," I interrupted, "she'll be downstairs with the little girls."

Celestine and I were in the seventh grade, which meant our room was on the top floor now, and also that we would wear special blue wool berets in choir. I was trying to remind Celestine that Mary was too young for our serious attention, but I made the mistake of not knowing what had happened last week, when Mary went into the school to take tests from Sister Leopolda.

"I'll be in your class," said Mary.

"What do you mean?" I said. "You're only eleven!"

"Sister put me ahead two grades," said Mary, "into yours."

The shock of it made me bend to my cookie cutting. She was smart. I already knew she was good at getting her way through pity. But smartness I did not expect, or going ahead two grades. I pressed the little tin cutters of hearts, stars, boys, and girls into the cookie dough. The girl shape reminded me of Mary, square and thick.

"Cousin Mary," I said, "aren't you going to tell Celestine what was in the little blue box you stole out of your mother's closet."

Mary looked right at me. "Not a thing," she said.

Celestine stared at me like I was crazy.

"The jewels," I said to Mary, "the rubies and the diamonds."

We looked each other in the eye, and then Mary seemed to decide something. She blinked at me and reached into the front of the dress. She pulled out the cow's diamond on a string.

"What's that?" Celestine was interested at once.

Mary displayed the wonder of how the light glanced through her treasure and fell, fractured and glowing, on the skin of her palm. The two of them stood by the window taking turns with the cow's lens, ignoring me. I sat at the table eating cookies. I ate the feet. I nibbled up the legs. I took the arms off in two snaps and then bit off the head. What was left was a shapeless body. I ate that up too. All the while I was watching Celestine. She wasn't pretty, but her hair was thick and full of red lights. Her dress hung too long behind her knees, but her legs were strong. I liked her tough hands. More than anything else, I liked her because she was mine. She belonged to me, not Mary, who had taken so much already.

"We're going out now," I told Celestine. She always did what I said. She came, although reluctantly, leaving Mary at the window.

"Let's go to our graveyard," I whispered. "I have to show you something."

I was afraid she wouldn't go with me, that she would choose right there to be with Mary. But the habit of following me was too strong to break. She came out the door without a backward look, leaving Mary to take the last batch of cookies from the oven.

We walked out to the graveyard.

"What do you want?" said Celestine when we stepped into the long secret grass. Wild plum shaded us from the house. We were alone.

We stood speechless in the hot silence, breathing air thick with dust and the odor of white violets. I didn't know what to do, or what to tell Celestine. She pulled a strand of grass and put the tender end between her lips. She waited.

Maybe if Celestine had quit staring, I wouldn't have done what I did. But she stood there in her too-long dress, and let the sun beat down on us until I thought of what to show her. My breasts were tender. They always hurt. But they were something that Mary didn't have.

One by one, I undid the buttons of my blouse. I took it off. My shoulders felt pale and fragile, stiff as wings. I took off my undervest and cupped my breasts in my hands.

My lips were dry. Everything went still.

Celestine broke the stillness by chewing grass, loud, like a rabbit. She hesitated just a moment and then turned on her heel. She left me there, breasts out, never even looking back. I watched her vanish through the bushes and then a breeze flowed down on me, riffling the cloth around my shoulders, passing like a light hand. What the breeze made me do next was almost frightening. Something happened. I turned in a slow circle. I tossed my hands out. I swayed as if I heard music from below. Quicker, and wilder, I lifted my angry feet. I began to tap them down and then I was dancing on their graves.

Mary Adare

How long was Sita going to shimmy there, I wondered, with her shirt half off and thunderclouds lowering? I heard Celestine walk into the kitchen below and bang the oven door open, so I came down. I stood in the kitchen watching her lift each cookie off the sheet with a spatula. She never broke one. She never looked up. But she knew I was there, and she knew that I'd been up on the second floor watching Sita take off her shirt. I knew that because she hardly glanced up when I spoke.

"It's dark all of a sudden," I said, "there's a storm."

"Sita's mother's going to worry," said Celestine, dusting flour off her hands. "I'll get her."

But before she was halfway across the yard Sita came, walked right past her, jumped on her bicycle and rode away. That is how I got caught in the rain that afternoon. It swept down in sheets while I still had a mile left to walk. I slogged in the back door of the house, stood dripping on the hemp mat.

Fritzie rushed at me with a thick towel and practically took my head off rubbing it dry.

"Sita! Get out here and apologize to your cousin," she hollered. She had to call Sita twice before she came, and when Sita did walk into the back hall, unrepentant, her apology held no hint of shame.

On the first day of school that next fall, we walked out of the door together, both carrying fat creamy tablets and new pencils in identical wooden pencil boxes, both wearing blue. Sita's dress was new with sizing, mine was soft from many washings. It didn't bother me to wear Sita's hand-me-downs because I knew it bothered her so much to see those outgrown dresses, faded and unevenly hemmed by Fritzie, diminished by me and worn to tatters, not enshrined as Sita no doubt wished.

We walked down the dirt road together and then, hidden from Fritzie's view by the short pines, we separated. Or rather, Sita ran long-legged, brightly calling, toward a group of girls also dressed in stiff new material, white stockings, unscuffed shoes. Colored ribbons, plumped in bows, hung down their backs. I lagged far behind. It didn't bother me to walk alone.

And yet, once we stood in the gravel schoolyard, milling about in clumps, and once we were herded into rows, and once Celestine began to talk to me and once Sita meanly said I'd come in on the freight train, I suddenly became an object of fascination. Popular. I was new in Argus. Everybody wanted to be my friend. But I had eyes only for Celestine. I found her and took her hand. Her flat black eyes were shaded by thick lashes, soft as paintbrushes. Her hair had grown out into a tail. She was strong. Her arms were thick from wrestling with her brother, Russell, and she seemed to have grown even taller than a month ago that summer. She was bigger than the eighth-grade boys, as tall as the tallest Sister, Leopolda, whom she could look in the eye.

We walked up the pressed rock stairs, following our teacher, a round-faced young Dominican named Sister Hugo. And then, assigned our seats in alphabetical order, I was satisfied to find myself in the first desk, ahead of Sita.

Sita's position soon changed, of course. Sita always got moved up front because she volunteered to smack erasers together, wash blackboards, and copy out poems in colored chalk with her perfect handwriting. Much to her relief, I soon became old hat. The girls no longer clustered around me at recess but sat by her on the merry-go-round and listened while she gossiped, stroked her long braid, and smirked to attract the attention of boys in the upper grade.

Halfway through the school year, however, I became famous. I didn't plan it or even try to cause the miracle, it simply happened one cold day late in winter, after a thaw.

Overnight that March, the rain had gone solid as it fell. Frozen runnels paved the ground and thick cakes of ice formed beneath the eaves where the dripping water solidified midair. We slid down the glossy streets on the way to school, but later that morning, before we got our boots and coats from the closet for the recess hour, Sister Hugo cautioned us that sliding was forbidden. It was dangerous. But once we stood beneath the tall steel slide outdoors, this seemed unfair, for the slide was more a slide than ever, frozen black in one clear sheet. The railings and steps were coated with invisible glare. At the bottom of the slide a pure glass fan opened, inviting the slider to hit it feet first and swoop down the center of the schoolyard, which was iced to the curbs.

I was the first and only slider.

I climbed the stairs with Celestine behind me, several boys behind her, and Sita hanging toward the rear with her girlfriends, who all wore dainty black gum boots and gloves, which were supposed to be more adult, instead of mittens. The railings made a graceful loop on top, and the boys and bolder girls used it to gain extra momentum or even somersault before they slid down. But that day it was treacherous, so slick that I did not dare hoist myself up. Instead, I grabbed the edges of the slide. My position was awkward. If I went down at all, it would have to be head first.

From where I crouched the ride looked steeper, slicker, more dangerous than I'd imagined. But I did have on the product of my mother's stolen spoons, the winter coat of such heavy material I imagined I would slide across the schoolyard on it as if it were a piece of cardboard.

I let go. I went down with terrifying speed. But instead of landing on my padded stomach I hit the ice full force, with my face.

I blacked out for a moment, then sat up, stunned. I saw forms run toward me through a haze of red and glittering spots. Sister Hugo got to me first, grabbed my shoulders, removed my wool scarf, probed the bones of my face with her strong, short fingers. She lifted my eyelids,whacked my knee to see if I was paralyzed, waggled my wrists.

"Can you hear me?" she cried, mopping at my face with her big manly handkerchief, which turned bright red. "If you hear me, blink your eyes!"

I only stared. My own blood was on the cloth. The whole playground was frighteningly silent. I was afraid to move. Then I understood my head was whole and that no one was even looking at me. They were all crowded in a circle at the end of the slide. Even Sister Hugo was standing there now, her back turned. When several of the more pious students sank to their knees, I could not contain myself. I lurched to my feet and tottered over. somehow, I managed to squeeze through their cluster, and then I saw.

The pure gray fan of ice below the slide had splintered, on impact with my face, into a shadowy white likeness of my brother Karl.

He stared straight at me. His cheeks were hollowed, his eyes dark. His mouth was held in a firm line of pain and the hair on his forehead had formed wet spikes, the way it always did when he slept or had a fever.

Gradually, the bodies around me parted and then, very gently, Sister Hugo led me away. She took me up the stairs and helped me onto a cot in the school infirmary.

She looked down at me. Her cheeks were red from the cold, like polished apples, and her brown eyes were sharp with passion.

"Father is coming," she said.

"I'm sorry, I'll take demerits," I promised abjectly.

"Don't try to talk," she said, and then popped quickly out.

As soon as she was gone, I jumped off the cot and went straight to the window. An even larger crowd had now collected at the base of the slide, and now Sister Leopolda was setting up a tripod and other photographic equipment. It seemed incredible that Karl's picture should cause such a stir. But he was always like that. People noticed him. Strangers gave him money while I was ignored, just like now, abandoned with my wounds. I heard the priest's measured creak on the stairs, then Sister Hugo's quick skip, and I jumped back.

Father opened the door and allowed his magnificence to be framed in it a moment while he fixed me with his most penetrating stare. Priests were only called in on special cases of discipline or death, and I didn't know which one this was.

He motioned to Sister Hugo, and she ducked from the room. He drew a chair up beneath his bulk and sat down. I lay flat, as if for his inspection. There was a long and uncomfortable silence.

"Do you pray to see God?" he asked finally.

"Yes," I said.

"Your prayers were answered," Father stated.

He folded his fingers into the shape of a church and bit harshly on the steeple, increasing the power of his stare.

"Christ's Dying Passion," he said. "Christ's face formed in the ice as surely as on Veronica's veil."

I knew what he meant at last, and so kept silent about Karl. The others at Saint Catherine's did not know about my brother, of course. To them the image in the ice was that of the Son of God.

As long as the ice on the playground lasted, I was special in the class again, sought out by Sita's friends, teacher, and even boys, who were drawn to the glory of my black eyes and bruises. But I stuck with Celestine. After the sliding, we were even better friends than before. One day the photographers came to school and I made a great commotion about not having my picture taken unless it was with her. We stood together in the cold wind, at the foot of the slide.

"GIRL'S MISHAP SHAPES MIRACLE" was the headline in the *Argus Sentinel*.

For two weeks the face was cordoned off and farmers drove for miles to kneel by the cyclone fence outside Saint Catherine's school. Rosaries were draped on the red slats, paper flowers, little ribbons, and even a dollar or two.

And then one day the sun came out and suddenly warmed the earth. The face of Karl, or Christ, dispersed into little rivulets that ran all through the town. Echoing in gutters, disappearing, swelling through culverts and collecting in basements, he made himself impossibly everywhere and nowhere all at once so that all spring, before the town baked hard, before the drought began, I felt his presence in the whispering and sighing of the streams.

Celestine James

I have a back view of Mary when she shoots down the slide to earth. Her heavy gray wool coat stands out like a bell around the white clapper of her drawers, but the wind never ruffles her blue scarf. She is motionless in her speed, until she hits. Then suddenly things move fast, everywhere, all at once. Mary rolls over twice. Blood drenches her face. Sister Hugo runs toward her and then there are screams. Sita draws attention to herself by staggering to the merry-go-round, dizzy at the sight of her cousin's blood. Like a tortured saint, maybe Saint Catherine herself, she drapes her body among the iron spokes at the center of the wheel, and calls out, in a feeble but piercing tone, for help.

I do not go to her. Sister Hugo is now leading Mary up the stairs with her handkerchief and the blue scarf pressed on Mary's forehead. I have backed down the iced-over slide like magic, and now I run after the two of them. But Sister Hugo bars me from the door once they reach the infirmary.

"Go back down," she says in a shaking voice. Her eyes blaze strangely underneath her square starched linen brow. "It may not last," she says, "run to the convent! Tell Leopolda to haul herself right over with the camera!"

I am confused.

"The ice, the face," says Sister Hugo frantically. "Now *get!*"

And so I run, so amazed and excited at how she has expressed herself, not like a teacher but just like a farmer, that I do not ring the convent bell but leap straight into the entryway and scream up the echoing stairs. By then I know, because it is in the air of the schoolyard, that some kind of miracle has resulted from Mary's fall.

So I shout A MIRACLE at the top of my lungs. To do that in a convent is like shouting FIRE in a crowded movie. They all rush down suddenly. Leopolda springs down last of all with a fearsome eagerness. A tripod is strapped on one shoulder. Drapes, lights, and a box camera are crammed in her arms. It is like she has been right behind her door, armed with equipment, praying year in and year out for this moment to arrive.

Back on the schoolground, all is chaos. A crowd has formed around the end of the slide. Later on, the face they stare at is included in the catechism textbooks as "the Manifestation at Argus," with one of Sister Leopolda's photographs to illustrate. In the article, Mary is described as "a local foundling," and the iced slide becomes "an innocent trajectory of divine glory." The one thing they never say in any of the textbooks is how Sister Leopolda is found several nights after Mary's accident. She is kneeling at the foot of the slide with her arms bare, scourging herself past the elbows with dried thistles, drawing blood. After that she is sent somewhere to recuperate.

But that day, in all the confusion, I sneak upstairs to the infirmary. As I walk down the hall Father comes out of the infirmary door. He is lost in serious thought and never lifts his head, so he does not see me. As soon as he is down the hall I slip straight in, alarmed because a priest near a sick person spells doom.

But Mary is recovered from the blow, I think at first, because she's sitting up.

"Did you see him!" she says immediately, clutching my arm. She looks deranged, either with her sudden importance or with the wound. Her head is taped in gauze now, which would give her a nun-like air except that her eyes are beginning to show black and purple bruises.

"They say it's a miracle," I tell her. I expect her to laugh but she grips my hand hard. Her eyes take on a glitter that I start to suspect.

"It was a sign," she says, "but not what they think."

"How do you mean?"

"It was Karl."

She has never mentioned Karl before, but from Sita I know he is her brother who has run off on a boxcar heading west.

"Lay back," I tell Mary. "You're not feeling well."

"He's got to bother me," she says loudly. "He can't leave me alone."

But her face screws up. She is thinking deeply like the priest and has lost all track of me or even of herself. Her eyes glare into the distance, light and still, and I see that she is very annoyed.

After Sister Hugo sends me out of the infirmary for the second time I walk down the stairs, out into the cold overcast weather, and join the throng clustered around the miraculous face. Only to me, it is not so miraculous. I stare hard at the swirls of frozen mud, the cracked ice, the gravel that shows through the ice, the gray snow. Other people looking from the same angle see it. I do not, although I kneel until my knees grow numb.

That night the miraculous face is all that Russell and my two sisters, Carole and Pauline, can talk about.

"Your girlfriend's going to put us on the map," declares Pauline. She's the oldest, taking care of us by holding down jobs with farmers, cooking and sometimes even threshing right along with the men. "Girls have been canonized for less," she now says. Pauline carries the banner in Saint Catherine's Procession every year, looking huge and sorrowful, but pure. My mother's name was Regina, like the English queen, and she was big, too, like all of us. It seems like I got all of my father's coloring, but am growing very quickly into my mother's size.

"I bet Sita's about ready to kill that little Mary," Russell says with a sharp laugh. Sita has made fun of him for being an Indian, and he is always glad to see her taken down a notch.

"They are taking a picture of Mary for the papers," I tell him. Carole and Pauline are impressed, but not Russell because he plays football and has been in the papers many times for making touchdowns. People say he is one Indian who won't go downhill in life, but will have success.

The next morning, before school starts, he comes with me to inspect the ice. During the night, someone has put up a low slat-and-wire fence around the sacred patch of ice.

He kneels by the fence and blesses himself. Then he walks his bicycle down the icy road to the high school. I am left at the bottom of the slide again, kneeling and squinting, even crossing my eyes to try and make the face appear. All the while the nuns are setting up the altar, right there in the schoolyard, for a special Mass. I begin to wish that I had asked Russell to point out the features for me exactly, so that I can see Christ too. Even now, I consider questioning the nuns, but in the end I don't have the courage and all through the Mass, standing with the seventh grade, watching Mary, Sita, Fritzie, and Pete take communion first, I pretend that I am moved by the smashed spot which is all I can see.

from *The Shooter*

Glen Martin

Peter Orr gazed into the depths of his beer; the carbonation os-
cillated upward, finally coalescing with the thin, milky foam. It
soothed him, as the four beers which he had consumed earlier
had soothed him. He was the only Shoshone in the entire Omo
Valley, and he needed some comfort, some solace. There were
Yuroks and Hupas who had migrated down from the Klamath,
and there were some Chumash and a couple of families of Paiutes.
And there were plenty of whites and Mexicans, of course. But he
was the only Shoshone, and so he allowed himself to be soothed
by beer.

There was a large window to the left of the bar, fly-specked
and distorted. The sky was bleeding to the end of the day in angry
gouts of red and yellow. Sunset in the Siskiyous. But a sunset more

violent than others. The world was burning up—all the world that mattered, at any rate—and the Omo Valley was right in the way of the encroaching conflagration.

The bartender was a thin, silvery man who flickered in and out of focus. He suffered from some dermatological disorder, and his skin peeled incessantly; not like a snake shedding its skin, which was a smooth process. Rather, it was like the untidy shedding of a deer, which changes the sienna coat of summer for the umber, thick one of winter. He had ventured north from San Francisco to open the bar, and for some reason he had not been chased out of town when his homosexuality became known; it was like a weak joke. One evening, as Orr had worked his way through several beers at the bar, the bartender had whispered to him. "Let's you and me do it," he had said. "It probably won't be any good, but let's do it anyway." Orr had laughed gently, prior to snapping the bartender suddenly and viciously on the nose; the bartender had yelped and flown backward. He was known as a great consumer of cocaine, and his septum was excruciatingly tender.

The bartender polished glasses calmly and with great concentration, as though he expected to find some enduring truth in smooth surfaces. The loggers and forest service employees filling the bar drank and looked out the window. Beyond the first ridge, ragged with firs and cedars, was the dull, angry glow of the fire.

The door to the bar opened. Leon Miller walked in, a man Orr disliked. Miller was Fire Management Officer for the Omo USFS Ranger District. Wan, rotund, he had a tiny, rosebud mouth which made Orr think of the assholes of young girls. Miller walked in and sat down next to Orr at the bar. He ordered a Coors; the bartender polished several glasses before he brought the beer to the bar, without a glass.

"I'll need a glass," Miller said.

The bartender gave Miller the one he was polishing. Orr did not look at Miller, but concentrated on the wonderful, luminous interior of his beer. Like Miller, he favored a glass.

"How'd it go today, Pete?" Miller asked, pouring his Coors carefully down the side of the glass.

"It went," Orr replied. "I cut line for sixteen hours." Orr was the lead sawyer on one of the line crews. He made over sixty dollars an hour on fires, which was even more than he made as one of the few top-fallers in the Omo Valley. Every logging outfit in the valley wanted Orr to cut for them. He had a gift with a chainsaw.

"We're going to have a hard time stopping that fucker," Miller said.

Orr nodded. "It might get into town."

"We'll have to stop in tomorrow," Miller continued. "We're going to go ahead with the big backfire show."

"I heard something about that."

"I'll need you to shoot tomorrow, Pete."

For the first time in their conversation, Orr looked directly at Miller; yet it was merely a sidelong scan of the FMO's face. Orr disliked what he saw in the eyes of most people.

"I'm a cutter, not a shooter," he said. "I don't like to shoot."

"I have plenty of cutters," Miller said. "I need shooters—the best I can find. You're the best in the valley. I got Wayne Peekner, Charlie Oakum, and the Corley brothers for the flanks. I need you for the point."

"Find somebody else." Orr examined his beer. "I cut. I don't shoot."

"You shoot tomorrow, or you don't work. This is my fire. I make the line assignments. I need shooters. I got plenty of cutters."

On large wildfires, something occurs which is so horrible that it must be seen before the horror may be fully comprehended. The fires burn with such ferocity that they generate vortices of flame; the front moves ahead with such speed that it looks like a rolling, cresting, incandescent surf. Animals cannot escape it. They burn, and burning, they run across the firelines which men are attempting to hold. They run across the lines into the unprotected brush and trees; and burning, they die there, kindling new fires. The line is lost, and the agonizing process of constructing a new line begins again. To prevent this, shooters are sometimes posted along the lines. As the burning animals stagger onto the line, they are shot.

"Okay," Orr said. "I'll shoot if you want to be a fuckhead about it. Shoot or cut, I guess it's all the same."

"Good." Miller drank his beer and walked out the door.

Orr awoke before dawn as he always did, and he got out of bed slowly. His head throbbed only slightly. He started a fire under the coffee, and showered in the small, cramped stall that took up most of his trailer's bathroom. Outside the window, his dog whined. Orr toweled himself off. The air was warm, dry as a husk. He drank the entire pot of coffee.

He decided to take the .264 with the 4x8 variable scope: his antelope gun. The rifle kicked like a mule and set his ears ringing every time he touched one off, but he could drive nails with it at 400 yards. He picked the weapon off the rack in the bedroom and sheathed it, then filled his pockets with cartridges.

Outside, the sky was an opalescent gray to the east and a rich, deep orange to the west. Needles of flame flickered like static electricity across the horizon. Orr climbed into his truck and drove toward the western sky.

The yellow shirts of the firefighters seemed almost painfully brilliant in the gray light. There were hundreds of them working on the line: running out hose lays, setting up portable reservoirs, driving engines into position. Several D-8 cats continued to widen the line, even though it was almost a quarter-mile in breadth. Though the head of the fire was still three miles away, it could be heard as a low, deep groan, a noise which seemed to be coming out of the earth itself. Ash fell like a spring snow flurry. Orr squatted in the soft, fluffy soil of the line, smoking cigarettes, his rifle supported between his knees. He thought of the ranch he had left years before on the reservation outside of Winnemucca. He thought of hunting sage hens. He would sit with his brothers around the reservoirs at dusk, and when the birds came sailing in for their evening drink, the brothers would knock them down with ease. They had no dog, so they made their youngest brother retrieve the birds when they fell into the water.

Miller approached Orr. He was attired in full Fire Boss regalia: yellow Nomex jumpsuit, duckbill hardhat, web gear festooned with fusee flares, napalm grenades, canteens and first-aid kit, a radio slung from his belt. The other shooters walked behind him. Orr rose slowly to his feet.

"Okay," Miller said. "We're all here. Once all the hose lays get in we'll start firing."

The shooters said nothing. Orr continued to smoke. Peekner put some Copenhagen into his mouth and offered the can to Oakum. The Corley brothers looked vacantly at the ground.

"You guys know what you're supposed to do," Miller continued, addressing all the shooters but Orr. "Why don't you get on up there? Pete, you follow me."

Miller began trudging up the line, and Orr walked slowly behind him. They stopped finally at a rock outcropping at the highest point of the line. A serpentine bluff rose directly behind them, and slightly to the east of that there was an expanse of second-growth fir, pine, oak, and manzanita stretching to the outskirts of the town. If the line was not held, Omo would burn. There was a small, spring-fed pond about a hundred yards into the brush below them, and Orr could see several pairs of wood ducks paddling about. He would be back in October with his twelve-gauge.

"This is it." Miller settled onto a rock. "You can cover around five hundred yards on each side."

"Good," Orr replied. "I can take it from here."

"I'll stay too." Miller gestured. "This is a great vantage point for me. I can see the whole show from here."

Orr lit another cigarette. The idea of spending the entire day with Miller vaguely nauseated him. Miller took a thermos from his pack and poured himself a cup of coffee. He glanced at Orr.

"Didn't you bring a lunch?"

"I don't like to eat in the middle of the day," Orr said. "It makes me sleepy."

Miller laughed and sucked at the coffee. "This is where we're going to stop her," he said. "I can feel it. There's going to be a promotion in this for me. I'll get a GS-14 and my own district."

"Great," Orr answered, watching as one pair of wood ducks leaped from the water and flew toward the town. The other ducks soon followed. Miller took the radio from his belt and began talking, ordering additional hose lays, telling the firing crews to take their positions, directing holding crews into the brush behind the lines so they could jump on any spot fires that slopped over, commanding the retardant bombers droning overhead to start their approaches for the first drops. Orr watched the little spotter plane lead the bombers in.

"Tell those planes not to bomb this position," Orr said. "I don't want any of that crap fouling my gun."

"I want them to saturate all the fuels behind the line," Miller answered.

"It won't hurt anything to miss us," Orr snapped, flaring abruptly in temper. "I didn't bring my best gun out here to get it sludged up."

"The Forest Service will buy you another gun. We replace any equipment lost by our contractors on fires. You know that."

"You can't replace this gun," Orr said. "It's an old model customized Remington. The best gunsmith in Portland made it when the .264 was still a wildcat caliber. You tell those boys to dump that crud somewhere else or I'm walking off this line, and you can take my wages and ram them up your fat ass."

"I don't have to take that shit from you," Miller answered, and when Orr didn't reply, he bent down to sit once again on his haunches and look down at the men laying out hoses and taking up positions.

Finally, Miller looked up again. "Okay," he said. "I need you to shoot. But you're going to change your tune if you ever want to work in this district again."

"Shove it," Orr said softly, lighting another smoke.

Miller got on his radio and directed the spotter plane to lead the bombers away from the serpentine bluff. The sun rose above the ridges, red and sullen through the smoke. The sound of the fire deepened as it drew nearer, and became a presence Orr felt with his flesh. The little spotter plane pirouetted as it dove over the line, and the lumbering DC-6s followed it, dropping thousands of gallons of retardant, a red slurry of bentonite, ammonium phosphate, iron oxide, and water. The color of the retardant was not a brilliant crimson, but a muddy off-shade, like old blood.

The firing crews began firing out the line with napalm grenades and fusees. The solid, muffled booming of the grenade concussions played an interesting counterpoint to the beating pulse of the head of the fire; and now the crackling of the backfire wove itself into the whole. Orr eased a cartridge from the magazine into the chamber of the .264 and flicked off the safety. Miller was babbling into the radio. To Orr, the radio codes sounded like some brutal shorthand language. He speculated on the numbers as he fumbled for another smoke. If you could just talk in numbers, you could save a lot of trouble. And time. You could say everything you had to say, and then you could get down to the real business of doing what you were doing—whatever that was. Drinking. Screwing. Teaching your kid how to drop a transmission. Making your little brother wade into the freezing waters of a desert reservoir in mid-November to retrieve a sage hen. Or maybe it was just English that bothered him. He still spoke the Shoshone dialects, and the French patois of the tribe. No, the words were okay. Numbers might be better, but Shoshone and French were okay. English was Okay. It was just that goddamned Miller he couldn't stand. He hated the words that came out of that pink little mouth.

Orr thought a bit about his past. His family had not been pleased when he'd left the ranch to log in Oregon and northern California. They had a place for him on the ranch. They had wanted him to study business administration at the University of Nevada. Their ranch was large, and they made money on their cow and calf operation, and they made money on their registered Hereford and Brangus operations, and they made money on their alfalfa operation. They had received a windfall allotment from the feds. Like all the rest, Orr had received some money. And when he didn't go home and plow his check back into the operation, he mother had written him a letter. It had been short:

Dear Son:

I've tried to understand you for the longest time, but I can't. You have opportunities here that any of the kids you grew up with would kill to have. But you don't care. You just throw it all away. Like you've just thrown your allotment away. You tell me you bought a new truck and then wrecked it like you tell me you might cut your finger or something. What's wrong with you? We all used to care about what's wrong with you, but we just can't anymore. I can't even say your name in front of your father. He gets so mad, and you know I can't blame him, Peter. We had problems with all you boys, but not like we had with you. Please don't write me or call me anymore. I've had it, Peter.

Your

Mom

The letter cut Orr in some dark, strange place, but his essential and truest reaction was one of relief. The letter freed him from his family, and his tribe. Now he was not Shoshone. Now he was Orr, and he was no more a part of any society than a rock in a rubble of scree.

A shot boomed from the southern sector of the line, then another.

"Looks like the Corleys got some action," Miller said. "Keep your eyes open."

The two men exchanged glances. The firing crews were obscured in the smoke they had created around themselves, and the crackling of the backfire had reached a manic, almost hysterical crescendo. There was a faint ghost, charcoal gray in the smoke, and Orr was instantly alert. The ghost quickened and took on the substance of flesh and hide. Orr lifted the gun and brought the scope to bear. It was a fat blacktail doe, and she was clean: not a hair of her was singed. She kicked nervously up and down the line for several moments before she bounded on pogo-stick legs across the breadth of the line and into the brush on the far side. A few seconds later, two yearlings—obviously spoiled, indulged fawns from the previous season who had elected to stay with a mother who had not bred that year—followed in her wake.

The smoke billowed down on them, acrid and resinous, and Orr heard the fire boss begin to cough as another ghost appeared out of the smoke. Again Orr scoped it, and saw a spike buck leaping frantically up the line, its hindquarters smouldering. Orr swung, placing the cross hairs just ahead of the chest as the deer quartered away from him at a distance of 250 yards. When he fired, the noise and shock of the .264 shook Orr to the bone. It always hurt him to shoot this gun; he was a large, well-muscled man, but anyone suffered who shot the .264. A .458 magnum cartridge necked down for a .26 caliber bullet exacts a price from the hunter as well as the hunted.

The buck's legs folded behind its body as if cut by a razor, and it dove nose first into the soil. Orr ejected the empty casing and put it into his pocket.

"That's the way." With the radio, Miller directed a crew to the deer. Orr watched as the yellow-shirted figures struggled with their hoses to the smoking animal, finally drenching it long and hard until it seemed a small, sad bundle of sodden fur devoid of bones.

"Yo!" Miller yelled, and Orr swung the gun to the south, in the direction of Miller's outstretched hand.

A badger dragged itself along the line less than a hundred yards distant, the pelt along its spine burning. The animal was so low to the ground that Orr's first shot did nothing more than throw up a geyser of dirt in front of it. His second shot, however, caught the badger directly behind the shoulder, and it lurched slowly into the air. Orr again ejected the casing, his mood becoming increasingly somber with each shot. Miller, however, was positively ebullient. Each animal that Orr shot, each shot from one of the other shooters down the line, inspired him to ever greater delight. His small, cornflower-blue eyes danced behind his thick spectacles, his red lips were moist as they worked against the microphone of the radio. The word from the spotter plane and the holding crews was positive. The line was secure, the backfire was pulling in a wonderfully symmetrical fashion to the head of the main fire. Miller, it seemed, would indeed get his GS-14 rating and his own district. Omo would be saved.

The sun was high now; Orr figured it was past ten o'clock. He sat on his heels and opened a fresh pack of Winstons. The sun was hot, and the perspiration soaking through his hickory shirt had a metallic tang to it. He sat with his head down, and let the sweat relieve him of old toxins and old concerns. His mother, his family; his tribe, the dogs he had owned throughout his thirty-four years; the women who had sometime made a difference, but never enough of a difference; the fires, the burning deer, this pompous fool sitting next to him, as though it was the most natural relationship in the world; he let it all work its way through his guts and out onto his skin, to streak his shirt with white minerals.

The column of backfire smoke pulled away from them, leaving the two men blinking in the white, hard light of a mountain summer morning. The column rose straight into the sky for several thousand feet, joining with the column from the main fire and flattening off at the top. Backfire and wildfire were one now, and the fires were starving themselves to death.

Orr stretched luxuriously, and his spine snapped like castanets. There was nothing to do now but wait until the flames had died completely, nothing to do but lounge around the line, putting off the final descent, knowing that dinner was irrevocably in the bag.

The bear materialized out of the smoke column abruptly. Orr was used to wildlife appearing suddenly in places which were empty mere microseconds earlier, with no discernible motion. Still, this shocked him. The animal which had come from the smoke was a grizzly bear: humpbacked, silver-tipped, dish-faced. A grizzly bear in black bear territory.

"There are no grizzlies in California," Orr thought. "There aren't any in Oregon. Nevada. Maybe one or two in the North Cascades in Washington. A couple in Idaho. Most in Montana and Wyoming. None in California."

The bear was on fire. Smoke curled from its flanks. It loped up the line toward them with a liquid, powerful piston-like stroking of its four huge limbs; like all bears, it moved with surprising speed and grace. Firefighters scrambled out of its way or were knocked over like barley before a scythe. The bear was intent on forward progress rather than mayhem, however, and none of the men appeared injured. A short, deep cough of pain and confusion drifted to Orr on the light wind. The sun glittered off the silver guard hairs of the bear's pelt.

It was one of those moments when time attenuated, and became cold and slow. Orr had time to contemplate the bear's probable journey from the Rocky Mountains of Montana to the precipitous coastal Siskiyous in California. It had probably crossed over from the Bitteroots into Idaho. Climbed the Great Divide. Maybe followed the Salmon River down to the Columbia. Hung out in Hell's Canyon for a time, until it became bored or hungry, and foraged southward. But how did it cross the Oregon desert? Not much to keep a griz alive there. Who the fuck knew? Somehow it got down to the upper Klamath, and from there it was a piece of cake. It could follow the river right down to the heart of the Siskiyous, and eat like a king on everything from acorns to camas to salmon to deer to garbage from the dumps of the little logging towns.

"Goddamn!" Miller screamed. "Shoot, you fucking moron!" The bear was running directly at them. It was no more than seventy-five yards away. Orr could see the cream-like spittle flecking its jaws, the huge, pink tongue. In another few yards he would be able to make out the small, bright, intelligent eyes, clouded with pain and fury. The gigantic slabs of muscle along the bear's spine and rump rippled under the golden fur. Christ! A grizzly in California! This was the most important day in Orr's life.

"Shoot! Shoot!" Miller screamed, his voice cracking and breaking as it climbed in register. "What's the matter with you, you fucking Indian? Shoot!"

Orr glanced briefly at Miller, whose face was contorted and red. He looked back to the bear, the gun gripped numbly in his left hand. The bear was almost on them now. Orr felt strangely joyous and at peace; he felt as he had at times felt as a young boy, when the vastness of life and its possibilities would inexplicably flood and fill him.

Miller grappled for the gun, no longer able to speak, his mouth working soundlessly. Orr tightened his grip on the .264 and pushed Miller away with his right hand. The FMO fell backward just as the bear was on them. It coughed in surprise, shortly and sharply, and Orr realized that the near sighted animal had not seen them until that moment. The collision with the bear lifted Orr several feet into the air, and he came down with a grunt on his left shoulder and thigh. The .264 pinwheeled as well, and landed on an outcropping of serpentine. Orr could hear the optics in the scope shatter, and he winced for the gun even through his pain. Strangely, Orr's eyes never left the bear. He watched it as time once again slowed. With a paw as large as a dinner plate, the bear pinned Miller to the ground, and in a long instant the great, shaggy head darted forward and the massive chops had snapped once before the bear moved on. It had never really paused in its flight.

Orr lay stunned in the dirt. Below him, Miller was moving, his limbs contracting and relaxing, his fingers clenching and unclenching. The body was almost decapitated. A fragment of vertebra gleamed whitely. Arterial blood jetted weakly from a severed carotid, and the head lay at a grotesque angle from Miller's body. His glasses were knocked off, the blue eyes open and glassy. Orr climbed painfully to his feet, and at that moment he heard a splash in the brush on the other side of the line. The bear had found the duck pond and was wallowing in the mud and algae at the far margin of the water, grunting in contentment. Orr could tell that the bear would live, that the burns were superficial. The animal had lost all sense of urgency, and it was now enjoying itself. Finally, with a great snort, it leaped from the pond and loped into the brush and was gone.

Orr was in pain as he looked at the path the bear had made through the brush. At two places along the path, smoke was twisting up toward the ringing blue sky. As Orr watched, pale flame vaulted up, hesitated, and then began ripping up the hill. The heat of the day had reached a crucial point; the fuels had yielded all their moisture some time before. The fire would not be stopped.

Making Do

from The Grace of Wooden Birds

Linda Hogan

1

Roberta James became one of the silent people in Seeker County when her daughter, Harriet, died at six years of age.

Harriet died of what they used to call consumption.

After the funeral, Grandmother Addie went to stay with Roberta in her grief, as she had done over the years with her children and grandchildren. Addie, in fact, had stayed with Roberta during the time of her pregnancy with Harriet, back when the fifteen-year-old girl wore her boyfriend's black satin jacket that had a map of Korea on the back. And she'd visited further back than that, back to the days when Roberta wore white full skirts and white blouses and the sun came in the door, and she lay there in that hot sun like it was ironed flat against the floor, and she felt good with clean hair and skin and singing a little song to herself.

There were oak trees outside. She was waiting. Roberta was wait-ing there for something that would take her away. But the farthest she got was just outside her skin, that black jacket against her with its map of Korea.

Addie never told Roberta a word of what she knew about divided countries and people who wear them on their backs, but later Roberta knew that her grandmother had seen way down the road what was coming, and warned her in little ways. When she brushed Roberta's dark hair, she told her, "You were born to a different life, Bobbie."

After the funeral, Roberta's mother offered comfort in her own way. "Life goes on," Neva said, but she herself had long be-longed to that society of quiet Indian women in Seeker, although no one would have guessed this of the woman who wore Peach Promise lipstick, smiled generously, and kissed the bathroom mir-ror, leaving a message for Roberta that said, "See you in the a.m. Love."

Grandma Addie tended Angela, Roberta's younger daughter. She fed the baby Angela spoonsful of meal, honey, and milk and held her day and night while Roberta went about the routines of her life. The chores healed her a little; perking coffee and clean-ing her mother's lipstick off the mirror. She swept away traces of Harriet with the splintered broom, picking up threads from the girl's dress, black hair from her head, wiping away her footprints.

Occasionally Neva stopped in, clasped her daughter's thin cold hands between her warm ones, and offered advice. "That's why you ought to get married," she said. She wrapped Roberta's shoul-ders in a large gray sweater. "Then you'd have some man to help when things are down and out. Like Ted here. Well, anyway, Honey," she said at eye level to Roberta, "You sure drew a good card when Harriet was born. Didn't she, Ted?"

"Sure sugar, an ace."

But when Roberta wasn't looking, Neva shook her head slowly and looked down at the floor, and thought their lives were all hopeless.

Roberta didn't get married like her mother suggested. She did take some comfort on those long nights by loving Tom Wilkins. Each night she put pieces of cedar inside his Red Wing boots, to keep him close, and neatly placed them beneath her bed. She knew how to care for herself with this man, keeping him close in almost the same space Harriet had abandoned. She wept slightly at night after he held her and he said, "There now. There now," and patted her on the back.

He brought her favorite Windmill cookies with him from town and he sang late at night so that the ghost of Harriet could move on more easily, like he eventually moved on when Roberta stopped placing cedar in his boots.

"Why didn't that Wilkins boy come back?" Grandma asked. "Choctaw, wasn't he?"

Roberta shrugged as if she hadn't left his boots empty of cedar. "He was prettier than me." She pushed her straggly hair back from her face to show Grandma what she meant.

A month later, Roberta was relieved when the company summoned Tom Wilkins to Louisiana to work on a new oil field and she didn't have to run into him at the store any longer.

Roberta's next child, a son she named Wilkins after the father, died at birth, strangled on his own cord. Roberta had already worn a dark shawl throughout this pregnancy. She looked at his small roughbox and said, "He died of life and I know how that can happen."

She held on to her grandmother's hand.

Grandma Addie and Neva talked about Roberta. "A woman can only hold so much hurt," Grandma said.

"And don't think I don't know it," said Neva.

Roberta surfaced from her withdrawal a half year later, in the spring of 1974, when Angela looked at her like a little grandmother and said, "Mother, I know it is hard, but it's time for me to leave you" and immediately became feverish. Roberta bathed her with alcohol and made blessing-root tea, which she dropped into little Angela's rose-petal mouth with an eye dropper. She prayed fervently to God or Jesus, she had never really understood which was which, and to all the stones and trees and gods of the sky and inner earth that she knew well, and to the animal spirits, and she carried her little Angel to the hospital in the middle of praying, to that house made of brick and window and cinders where dying bodies were kept alive, carried the girl with soft child skin in a small quilt decorated with girls in poke bonnets, and thought how funny it was to wrap a dying child in such sweetness as those red-cheeked girls in the calico bonnets. She blamed herself for ignoring Angela in her own time of grief. Four days later Angela died, wearing a little corn necklace Roberta made, a wristlet of glass beads, and covered with that quilt.

"She even told Roberta she was about to die," Neva told Ted. "Just like an old woman, huh, Bert?"

Roberta went on with her silence through this third death, telling herself over and over what had happened, for the truth was so bad she could not believe it. The inner voice of the throat spoke and repeated the words of loss and Roberta listened hard. "My Angel. My Harriet. All my life gone and broken while I am so young. I'm too young for all this loss."

She dreamed of her backbone and even that was broken in pieces. She dreamed of her house in four pieces. She was broken like the country of Korea or the land of the tribe.

They were all broken, Roberta's thin-skinned father broken by the war. He and Neva raised two boys whose parents had "gone off," as they say of those who come under the control of genie spirts from whiskey bottles, and those boys were certainly broken. And Neva herself who had once been a keeper of the gates; she was broken.

In earlier days she read people by their faces and bodies. She was a keeper of gates, opening and closing ways for people to pass through life. "This one has been eating too much grain," she'd say, or "That one was born too rich for her own good and is spoiled. That one is broken in the will to live by this and that." She was a keeper of the family gates as well. She closed doors on those she disliked, if they were dishonest, say, or mean, or small. There was no room for smallness in her life, but she opened the doors wide for those who moved her slightly, in any way, with stirrings of love or pity. She had lusty respect for belligerence, political rebellion, and for vandalism against automobiles or businesses or bosses, and those vandals were among those permitted inside her walls.

And now she was broken, by her own losses and her loneliness.

Roberta cried against Addie's old warm shoulder and Grandma Addie stayed on, moving in all her things, cartons of canning jars, a blue-painted porcelain horse, her dark dresses and aprons, pictures of her grandchildren and great-grandchildren, rose-scented candles of the virgin of Guadalupe, even though she was never a Catholic, and the antlers of the deer.

Roberta ignored her cousins from the churches of the brethren of this and that when they came to comfort her in their ways, telling her that all things were meant to be and that the Lord gives and takes.

Uncle James was older and so he said nothing, and she sat with him, those silent ones together.

Roberta's mother left messages on the bathroom mirror. "There is a time for everything in heaven."

With Grandma there to watch over Neva and the house, Roberta decided one day to pack her dishes, blankets, and clothes into the old Chevy she had bought from Ted, and she drove away from the little square tombstones named Angela, Wilkins, and Harriet, though it nearly broke her heart to leave them. She drove away from all those trying to comfort her with what comforted them. The sorrow in her was like a well too deep for young ground; the sides caved in with anger, but Roberta planned still to return for Grandma Addie. She stopped once, in the flat, neutral land of Goodland, Kansas, and telephoned back.

"You sure you don't want to come with me? It's kind of pretty out this way, Grandma," she lied. She smelled truck exhaust from the phone booth and she watched the long, red-faced boys walking past, those young men who had eaten so much cattle they began to look like them.

"Just go and get settled. I'll be out to visit as soon as you get the first load of laundry hung on the line."

Roberta felt her grandma smile. She hung up the phone and headed back to the overloaded, dusty white car.

She headed for Denver, but wound up just west of there, in a mountain town called The Tropics. Its name was like a politician's vocabulary, a lie. In truth, The Tropics was arid. It was a mine town, uranium most recently. Dust devils whirled sand off the mountains. Even after the heaviest of rains, the water seeped back into the ground, between stones, and the earth was parched again. Still, *Tropics* conjured up visions of tall grasses in outlying savannas, dark rivers, mists, and deep green forests of ferns and trees and water-filled vines. Sometimes it seemed like they were there.

Roberta told herself it was God's acres, that it was fate she had missed the Denver turn-offs from the freeway, that here she could forgive and forget her losses and get on with living. She rented a cabin, got a part-time job working down at the Tropics Grocery where she sold single items to customers who didn't want to travel to town. She sold a bag of flour to one, a can of dog food to another, candy to schoolchildren in the afternoon. She sold boxed doughnuts and cigarettes to work crews in the mornings and 3.2 beer to the same crews after five. She dusted and stacked the buckling shelves, and she had time to whittle little birds, as her Uncle James had done. She whittled them and thought of them as toys for the spirits of her children and put them in the windows so the kids would be sure and see them. "This one's for Harriet," she'd tell no one in particular.

When she didn't work she spent her time in bed, completely still and staring straight at the ceiling. They used to say if a person is motionless, their soul will run away from the body, and Roberta counted on that. They say that once a soul decides to leave, it can't be recalled. Roberta lay in that room with its blue walls and blue-flowered blanket. She lay there with her hair pulled back from her round forehead. She held the sunbonnet quilt in her hands and didn't move.

To her disappointment, she remained alive. Every night she prayed to die and join her kids, but every morning she was still living, breathing. Some mornings she pulled at her flesh just to be certain, she was so amazed and despairing to be still alive.

Her soul refused to leave. It had a mind of its own. So Roberta got up and began a restless walking. There were nights in

The Tropics that she haunted the dirt roads like a large-shouldered, thin-hipped ghost, like a tough girl with her shoulders held high to protect her broken heart. Roberta Diane James with her dark hair that had been worn thin from the hours she spent lying down trying to send her soul away. Roberta, with her eyes the color of dark river water after a storm when the gold stirs up in it. The left eye still held the trace of a wink in it, despite the thinness of skin stretched over her forehead, the smell of ivory soap on her as she tried over and over to wash the grief from her flesh.

2

When I first heard how bad things were going for Roberta, I thought about going home, but I heard my other voices tell me it wasn't time. "There is a season for all things," Mom used to say, and I knew Mom would be telling Roberta just that, in her own words, and that Roberta would be fuming inside as I had done with Mom's fifty-cent sayings.

I knew this much: Roberta would need to hold on to her grief and her pain.

Us Chickasaws have lost so much we hold on to everything. Even our muscles hold on to their aches. We love our lovers long after they are gone, better than when they were present.

When we were girls, Roberta and I saved the tops of Coke bottlecaps and covered them with purple cloth like grapes. We made clusters of grapes sitting out there on the porch, or on tire swings in the heat, and we sewed the grapes together. We made do. We drank tea from pickle jars. We used potato water to starch our clothes. We even used our skinny dark legs as paper for tic-tac-toe. Now the girls turn bleach containers into hats, cutting them in fours and crocheting them together.

Our Aunt Bell is famous for holding on and making do. There's a nail in her kitchen for plastic six-pack rings, a box for old jars, a shelf or box for everything, including all the black and white shoes she's worn out as a grown woman. Don't think those boxes or nails mean she's neat, either. She's not. She has hundreds of dusty salt and pepper shakers people gave her, and stacks of old magazines and papers, years of yellowed history all contained in her crowded rooms, and I love her for it, for holding on that way. I have spent hours of my younger life looking at those shakers and reading those papers. Her own children tell her it is a miracle the viruses of science aren't growing to maturity in there.

We save ourselves from loss in whatever ways we can, collecting things, going out to Danceland, getting drunk, reading westerns or finding new loves, but the other side of all this salvation is that we deny the truth. When some man from town steals our land, we say, "Oh, he wouldn't do that. Jimmy Slade is a good old boy. I knew his folks. I used to work for the Slades during the depression." Never mind that the Slades were not the hungry ones back then.

Some of us southern Indians used to have ranches and cattle. They were all lost piece by piece, or sold to pay for taxes on some land that was also lost. Now and then someone comes around and tells us we should develop our land like we once did. Or they tell us just to go out in the world. We nod and smile at them.

Now and then some of us young people make a tidal wave in the ocean of our history, an anxiety attack in the heart monitor of our race. We get angry and scream out. We get in the news. We strip ourselves bare in the colleges that recruited us as their minority quota and we run out into the snowstorm naked and we get talked about for years as the crazy Indian that did this or that, the one that drove to the gas station and went on straight to Canada, the girl who took out the garbage and never turned and went back. We made do.

I knew some people from up north. You could always tell they were from north because my friend's daughter had a walleye with a hook tattooed on her forearm. Once we went to a powwow together and some of the women of the People wore jingle dresses, with what looked like bells. "What are those?" I asked my friend.

They were snuff can lids. Those women of the forests and woodlands, so much making do just like us, like when we use silver salt cans in our dances instead of turtle-shell rattles. We make music of those saltshakers, though now and then some outsider decides we have no culture because we use store-bought shakers and they are not traditional at all.

I defy them: Salt is the substance of our blood, sweat, our secretions, our semen. It is the ocean of ourselves.

Once I saw a railroad engineer's hat in a museum. It was fully beaded. I thought it was a new style like the beaded tennis shoes or the new beaded trucker's hats. But it was made in the late 1800s when the Lakota* were forbidden to make traditional items. The mothers took to beading whatever was available, hats of the engineers of death. They covered colony cotton with their art.

We make art out of our loss.

That's why when I heard Roberta was in Colorado and was carving wooden birds, I figured it made sense. Besides, we come from a long line of whittlers and table carvers, people who work with wood, including the Mexican great grandfather who made santos and a wooden mask that was banned by the priests. Its presence got him excommunicated.

Uncle James carves chains out of trees. We laugh and say it sounds like something *they* would do.

Roberta was carving wooden birds, crows, mourning doves, and even a scissortail or two. She sent some of the birds back home to have Aunt Bell put them on the graves of her little ones.

I think she was trying to carve the souls of her children into the birds. She was making do.

*The People

Set

N. Scott Momaday

Set?

   The reflection in the glass is the transparent mask of a man. I am that man. It is my face, mine. I love my face. I love it because it is mine and because I have looked at it and touched it with my hands for many years; I have studied and memorized my face. Oh, it has changed—it changes—but, always, it is like no other face. And now I wonder at this ruse of light and shadow, this cold insinuation of myself. After all, there is so little to it, this pale, watered-down image. I cannot see the pits and pocks and stubble of my face. But the image is well made. It is as clean and essential as a line drawing by Hokusai, as delicate and tentative as the deer of Lascaux. And I wish that I had made it, for I am an artist, too, like Hokusai and like the one whose hand described the deer. Glass. Glass ought not confound the artist. When I was a boy, eight or nine years old, I ran through a glass door, therefore this—but it is not visible in the glass—white line in the brow of the right eye; you, there, your *left* eye.

Are you Set?

The glass seems a block of ice, hard, luminous, translucent, the image fixed deep within like a fossil. Fossil face. Set, Setman. No. It reminds me of . . .; once I saw a lithograph by the Dorset artist Jamasie. It was entitled, I think, *Igloo Builders Frightened by Bear.* And in it there were blocks of ice, finely striated, informed with a lucent smoke like this. The bear was lean and lithe, its body long like a weasel's. Ice bear, long and lean, Nanook, dog of God, old man with a fur cloak. Art, whatever it is, a profound intelligence of some sort, hand and eye bringing the imagination down hard upon the picture plane: and in this a nearly perfect understanding of the act of understanding—Ha! like someone looking into a glass at someone looking into a glass—transmitted to the fingertips, an understanding not of ice or bears or fright, but of these and more as a whole. Just now I brought the tips of my fingers together, the thumb and the forefinger and the middle finger of my right hand, your left, and I imagined that I drew water, faintly, faintly colored, across a porcelain plane with a brush, a very fine brush. My father had such a brush. His brushes were soft and sharp as needles. Sable. I used to twirl the sable hair in my fingers and wonder at the soft resiliency of the minute strands, that they should form and hold such a nearly perfect point. How, with something of so little resistance as fur, could my father make a line like the trace of a very hard, very sharp pencil along a rule's edge? There is no edge to this image in the glass—but how can that be?—and there is only one eye. And, what?—there is no grain of light in the eye, no spark of life! Yet it is a living eye. Look, I can move it in my head; ah, but I cannot see that I do so, that's the thing. It isn't funny; then why do I laugh? Why do I lock the joints in my feet, trying to press my weight down into the floor, trying to project my whole face into view?

You, Set?

Yes, I am Set.

And there, on the other side of the glass, is a hallway. The wall opposite is of a rough, darker-than-cream-colored texture, porous as pumice or ancient bone, or so it appears. My focus cannot hold upon my reflected face; suddenly it extends to the wall beyond like a shot; then it snaps back upon the glass, the cyclops there, the still, vacant eye.

Set, then.

Set.

Nod, damn you! The eye narrows a bit, but it remains fixed, seeming to see. I turn, feeling a resistance in the dank air. And the room darkens directly. The rain, which has been holding off all day—one day, two, several?—comes down hard and loud, driving, glancing, with wind. When my hearing is adjusted to the sharp, uneven rattle of the rain I realize that the telephone has been ringing in the next room, that the ringing has stopped, that the telephone had been ringing for a long time. I look through the crack in the door, and there is the black silence of a cave, a silence dense, almost palpable, enveloped in rain.

The image on the glass dissolves. Night comes with the rain, in the same instant. Everything in the studio is at once indistinct, save for the few canvases that stand about. It's strange, the large one, the one I have only just begun, is more obscure than the others. They stand out somewhat. They are bare and almost bright in the vague light, rectangles more or less sharply defined, glowing in the texture of fine white sand or polished rice. That one, though, the large one fixed to the fork of the easel, at eye level, under the skylight—that one is remote. It bewilders me. I ought to see, at least know, what is there. Didn't I work on it today, this morning? On the skylight an intermittent play of colors from the street lamps and the traffic lights and the cars below, and the caroms of rain, each drop exploding into color on the panes. And I cannot see or even remember what is there on the picture plane. There are not whorls of color, not now; there are only stains, deep and indefinite, in the flashes of yellow, white, blue, green, orange, red light. And I want to believe that there are real forms there, unique, intricate forms straightly related to a deep field of receding grounds, one after another, ranging to a black infinity, the definite forms of definite things, wonderful and unspeakable things, the very things that astonish God.

The telephone is ringing in the next room. No, it has rung; it has been ringing.

Lola?

Bent?

Jason, you?

Hello. Is someone there?

I think of going out. I take a step toward the cave. My legs are stiff and numb. I've been too long here in this room. I clear my throat. I must be sure that I can speak, for the phone will ring again, surely. I have not spoken a word all day, not aloud, is that possible?—not a word to a living soul. The rain is steady now, unrelenting. The luminous linen planes shimmer, and I take up the telephone, dead as a stone, and place it to my ear—

A moment ago I thought of going out. I don't mind getting out in the rain. I know, I ought to be hungry, but I don't feel hunger. Thirst. I need a drink. What a light show there at the window! The storm makes brilliant the colored grounds, the successive distances, rising into the night: blinking points of light, wavy lines of light, angles and curves of light, light of every color and intensity. And closer by it is dark, except the soft, spangled pools in which the rain spatters beneath the streetlamps, and deserted. Only now and then someone steps from a doorway on Fillmore Street, opens an umbrella, and disappears into the roiling vapors. And the Bay is black—

Hello. Set.

My ear is stopped, and there is nothing but the buzzing in my brain. Then, after long moments the crackle of the storm, then voices so far away as to be unintelligible.

Set here.

Set.

Set imagines it is to please, but it is to astonish God that he paints. His presumption and arrogance are monstrous and deadly, for they shall certainly lead to the Sin of Despair. Rather, as he himself says on occasion, he paints in vain, in order to relieve the boredom of God. He expounds: God's boredom is infinite. Surely we humans, even with our manners and our institutions and our in-laws, ceased to amuse Him many ages ago. What sustains Him is the satisfaction, deeper than we can know, of having created a few incomparable things—landscapes, waters, birds and beasts. He takes a particular pride in the stars, and it pleases him to breathe havoc upon the seas. He sighs to the music of the desert at dawn. The eagle and the whale give Him still to wonder and delight. And so must He grieve for the mastodon and the archaeopteryx. And the bear, ah, He used both hands when he made the bear. Imagine a bear proceeding from the hands of God!

Set remembers:

The boy Locke Lasker Setman, called Loki, thirteen, sat in a green leather chair in the living room of the Sandridge house on Scott Street. He peered hard into the book in his hands, even when the blue Great Dane Luke, called Luki, heaved and stretched, one massive forepaw nearly upsetting the fireplace screen, and yawned awesomely, emitting a whine that set the walls vibrating. The book was an illustrated astronomy, a text for common or public schools, published in New York in 1849. It was in bad repair, and Loki appreciated the need to handle it with care. It was fragile and the more dear to him for that. He had brought it down from Bent's study after breakfast, and for more than an hour he pored over it, especially the illustrations, indeed especially one, tracing the signs of the Zodiac with a forefinger. He was a Taurus; Bent had told him so one Sunday afternoon when the two of them had taken the ferry to Tiburon and Loki had broken a bagel and tossed the pieces up to the wheeling gulls. In the illustration the bull leapt lightly in the earth's orbit, strictly enclosed in its constellation under the legend, "OCTOBER," The Earth enters Taurus 23d October and at the same time the sun enters Scorpio." The book appeared to be a mine of irrefutable information, and Loki was fascinated with it. He imagined that he was back in the Peter and Paul Home, before his adoption, standing easily at his classroom desk, holding the tall, sloe-eyed Sister Stella Francesca in his benign regard, her incredulity and the perturbation of his peers hanging lightly like the scent of laurel about his head.

Q. What is the largest telescope in the world?

A. Lord Rosse's telescope, at Birr Castle, Ireland, 56 feet in length.

Q. What idea had the Ancients respecting the shape of the earth?

A. They believed it was an extensive plain, rendered uneven by hills and mountains.

Q. What is the distance of the sun from the earth?

A. It is about 95,000,000 of miles.

Q. How much greater is the equatorial than the polar diameter?

A. About 27 miles.

Q. What do the milky way and the single stars that are visible to the naked eye, including our sun, constitute?

A. They constitute an immense cluster, or firmament, entirely distinct from the other clusters or nebulae of the heavens.

Q. What is the shape of this great cluster or firmament?

A. It has the form of a wheel of burning-glass.

This image, holy and kaleidoscopic, brought tears to Loki's eyes. He saw in his imagination a great, glittering ring, or a succession of rings, spiraling through convolutions without number to a point on the far side of time. It was his first real notion of infinity; it struck and staggered him, and then, by the grace of God, it escaped his attention entirely. The information he relished most was this:

URSA MAJOR, the GREAT BEAR,—The first seven stars in this constellation form what is called the Great Dipper. It is situated about 15 degrees north of the zenith, and a little to the east of north. . . . There are four stars which form the dipper, and three in the Tail of the Bear, which form the handle. These stars cannot fail to be recognized at a glance. Six of these stars are of the second and one of the third magnitude. The first two, α, β, are called pointers, as a line drawn through them towards the horizon would pass very near the North Star, which is about 30 degrees from them towards the horizon.

And Set remembers:

The sun struck through the Scott Street windows, through an intricate floral pattern of stained glass. The light lay in four colors on Loki's hair and face. Even in sleep he was somehow sensible of the colored light; pale washes ran, one upon another, in back of his eyes. He dreamt of someone approaching, a frail young woman, her mouth, like Sister Stella Francesca's, set never to smile, her eyes holding on to something beyond his dream. And the dream was, is, always immediate. There is a rude, round rhythm to her walk. Her hair, dark and reddish, ripples as she comes. Her breasts are taut, and yet they bob and bounce, their motion slow and exaggerated. Her thighs are full, and they articulate the ivory-colored skirt of thin, raw silk, the ride and sway thereof, therein, far beyond his understanding; and yet he could not be more receptive, more alarmed or involved. She looks at him directly, neither with recognition nor without. Then she tosses her head, the thick hair swings across her mouth; it is for his benefit alone, this small, fastidious performance, and he winces. She is more than beautiful; she is extraordinarily graceful and sensual and alive; there is nothing about her that is not definitively feminine, and even on his precarious, adolescent terms she is wholly desirable in her flesh. At last she stands directly before him, over him, her feet set wide apart, and, shy and unaccountably ashamed, he hangs his head. Nevertheless he regards with a terrible excitement her shapely, sandalled feet, her long, painted toes.

And he dreams of making love to his mother. It is not unnatural, and there is no question of right and wrong; it is merely the irresistible accumulation of experience. Moreover, it is understood and accepted—neither is there any question of condonation—by the onlookers who are gathered with hard, intense interest about the altar. Among them he recognizes only his father, who smiles and proffers silent yet substantial encouragement. "Here, Loki," his mother says. "Here, darling, look." Only later, with his first woman, does the dream proceed beyond the blind of his innocence, beyond the frustration that is like paralysis. More fascinated than afraid, he looks into the dark recess, so sharply described upon the white mound of the woman's belly, and sees therein the ragged ridge of pink and magenta flesh protruding, almost discreetly, from the crisp, silky hair.

He awoke with alarm, a sour taste in his mouth, something like the taste of a grapefruit seed. Luke, Luki, lumbered to his feet, to the call of nature, and yawned mightily. Loki opened his eyes. Bent was standing on the third step of the stairs, looking at him. Bent's gray hair was forever tousled, and he squinted through little round, wire-rimmed glasses. He wore, as usual, the oversized, shapeless black cardigan with its many years of snags. He affected a stern stance, and the squint shaped a certain mask of irritability on his round, red face, but he was a gentle man.

"His Blue Eminence would seem to require a romp on the Green," said Bent. "Want to come along?"

Loki rubbed his eyes and nodded yes.

"Oh, and Señora Archuleta says would you like the salmon chowder for supper?"

Already Loki had got the scent of sizzling onions and salt pork, and he nodded yes again. It was a formality, question and nod. He loved Señora Archuleta's salmon chowder above all other dishes, save one—Señora Archuleta's Christmas posole.

Loki laughed to watch Bent work Luki on the leash. There was a boundless exuberance in the great blue animal, and an equal appetite for mischief. It seemed at times that he meant to do Bent in, giving him in a bound the line to hang himself, as it were, bounding abruptly into traffic, spinning him on the edges of curbs, stairs, piers, and platforms as he, Luki, lunged after cats and kids. But later, on the way back, when he had run himself into the ground, Luki was placid as a mule. And Loki held the leash with both hands, grateful to be assisted on the long, steep grade.

In Loki there was a certain empty space, a longing for something beyond memory. He thought often of his mother, dead almost the whole of his life. He knew she was not the pale, lewd ghost of his dreams; she was the touchstone to his belief in the past. Without knowing her, he knew of her having been; she had given him life, even as he had taken hers; her blood pulsed upon his heart. Her reality was that of everything on the bygone side of his existence. She was his immediate and most personal antecedent, the matter of which he was made. He could imagine her in a way no one else ever could.

When he opened the door on Scott Street there was a tumultuous outpouring of *Carmen,* Señora Archuleta's favorite music. The walls shivered, as with one of Luki's yawns. Bent, puffing, mumbled something from the walk below.

from *Raven's Road*

Paula Gunn Allen

Chapter I

In the deepness of night, two women sat under the crystal stars. They sat on the ground, looking at each other across a fire that cast uncanny shadows on their faces. They had sat so for hours, talking, gazing, murmuring, looking, occasionally expressing wonder, or shock, or amusement at what they could see.

In the firelight's reaching shadows they gazed upon one another, and learned all there was to know, each about each. When they had known and would know, what they had shared, what had happened over the millennia they had known one another, had not known one another, over the ages and ages they had been to one another everything human beings could be, and some things they could not. Now, in the black stillness before the night turns toward dawn, they sat in silence, each one contemplating in wonder her exhaustion, her exhilaration.

The one with the flat, broad face, deeply bronzed skin, and graying hair reached across the dying fire, offering her broad, square hand to her friend. "Come on, Eddie Raven," she said, her voice low with fatigue and fierce with love. "Let's go to bed."

The other, a tall, rangy woman whose skin was the color of a dusky rose, took the offered hand and drew herself easily to her feet. She yawned loudly, then stepped over the coals and took the shorter woman in her arms. "Allie, my dear, we've seen some times together." She leaned to kiss the forehead of the woman whose eyes glinted in the dying firelight, and, arms wound around each other, they made their way to the small tent pitched a short way from the fire.

They took off their boots and jackets and crawled into the double sleeping bag that nearly filled their tent. As Allie pulled Raven closer to her so that her head rested snugly on her shoulder, Raven said grumpily, "What time does that danged blast go off?"

Allie grinned in the dark. "Early. So better sleep fast!"

In a couple of hours she was shaking Raven. "Up, up. Morning calls. And such a morning you've hardly seen before. Come on, girl, let's hit the trail."

Raven sat up. Her barely opened eyes looked blankly at Allie. "Who are you?" she said crossly. "And what are you doing here?"

"I'm putting on my boots, my little chickadee, and my eagle-emblazoned jean jacket, which while not warm is splendid, don't you think?"

"Think? At this hour? Oh why oh why did I have to take up with a crazy Cheyenne," Raven looked skyward dramatically. "My mother tried to warn me, but would I listen? Oh, no, not me. Now here I am, in the middle of the mountains in the wilds of Nevada, about to go with my true love to see what I'm sure will sere my sight for good." Grumbling, she pulled on her boots and reached for her own jacket, a good quality wool mackinaw, almost new. She was vaguely conscious of its contrast to her girlfriend's frayed and pale Levi jacket. "Whither thou goest, indeed," she mumbled as she shrugged it on, "That woman was nuts, if you ask me! Haven't you heard that this might be dangerous, to watch atomic bombs go off?"

Allie reached out in the dark and patted the younger woman's head soothingly. "Now don't fret," she said. "It's no more dangerous than booze, dope, fast cars, or any of the white man's other civilized goodies. Besides," she chuckled as she unzipped the tent and stepped outside, "a warrior is expected to face danger bravely, like a brave. What's a little more death to us, aay?"

The women walked at a brisk pace along a dark trail that rose gently from their camp toward the east. They had about a two-mile trek through the rocky heights of the mountains above Yucca Flats. Allie had insisted that Raven join her on one of her bomb-watching expeditions, explaining that she felt a connection to the blasts, an obligation. She was waiting for something to happen, she said, something to come from them, though what had come so far was way off the mark. Still, she had said, it wasn't for her to understand; she had a job of a sort, and it was up to her to do it.

Raven had understood more than she knew. It was as though her muscles and chest comprehended the nature of Allie's job. Her thoughts, as far as she could tell, weren't in on the information, but being accustomed to acting in response to sources of knowing that went deeper than words or ideas, she had accepted easily Allie's invitation—well, her demand, really. Allie's insistence had been plain. Maybe that was what moved her, she thought now as they moved soundlessly over the ground. She reached into her pocket to make sure that her offerings were there. Whatever this morning brought, she was prepared to treat it with honor and respect.

After a half hour or so of rapid walking, Allie climbed a small peak and sat down, tucking her legs securely under her butt while Raven settled herself nearby. Reaching into the small canvas pack she was carrying, Allie took out two pairs of heavily colored goggles. "We're several miles from the blast," she said, "but I always wear these. No harm in being cautious." She handed Raven a pair. "They should be near ready," she said after a time. "They've gotten pretty efficient at this. You know what they say, 'practice makes perfect!' " They laughed quietly at her joke at the white man's expense.

As the sky caught fire in its customary way of awakening, Allie stood and walked to the edge of the peak. She raised the binoculars she was wearing and studied the plain below for a few moments. "I think they're about ready. Let's have a smoke and then gear up." She took two cigarettes from a pack of Lucky Strikes and lit them, handing one to Raven who had come up behind her. "Lookit that sky!" Allie exclaimed as she exhaled.

"Yep, it's really something," Raven replied. They smoked companionably for a few moments, watching the sun make its way above the horizon.

Abruptly, Allie reached into her pocket and drew out her goggles. "On your mark," she said in a jesting tone.

"All set," Raven responded, her calm voice belying the strange sensation she had of something writhing upward through her body and almost sensuously wrapping itself around her throat. She dropped her cigarette and ground it carefully into the stony dirt. They stood, hardly breathing, shoulders just touching in the growing winter light.

It was blotted out shortly by a sudden blast of light, a cloud, a mushroom cloud, a ball of light that rose and rose impossibly huge, impossibly bright—in spite of the protection of the dark, dark goggles. As Raven stood, transfixed, she realized that her eyes were shut tight and still she could see. Reflexively, she put her hand before her eyes, to shield them, and impossibly she could see through it, could see the bones of it eerily floating in her view. She couldn't breathe, couldn't name her feeling, fear or exhilaration, felt herself lifted outside of herself, felt herself soaring, suspended in the heights of the vast cloud that was still rising and billowing out over the plain.

What must it be like to be in it, she thought, what must it be like! Dizzy with the thought, feeling herself tumbling, tumbling, whited out, vaporized. "To go like that!" she managed to say aloud. "To become a particle of light!"

Beside her, Allie let her breath out in a small explosion, but said nothing. She put her arm around Raven, drawing her close.

They stood like that for a long time, until the cloud had begun to dissipate, until the winds were dying down. "Watch the fireball," she finally said, gravely. "Watch the fireball."

Turning to Raven then, Allie saw that she was making an offering to the cloud that still roiled, giving off brilliant striations of light, over them. She waited until her friend was done and had put away her pouch.

"Did you know that they take guys out to watch that close up?" she said. "They tell them, 'Watch the fireball!' They're lots closer to the blast than we are, by a long shot. I can just imagine what it's like to be there, and believe me, I only want to just imagine it." She took Raven's hand in hers and held it, looking down at it while she thought. She noticed again the strange deep mark on the back of the hand she held in hers, wondered again at the clarity of the imprint on it; it looked exactly like a wild strawberry. So exact was it that she had asked Raven if it had been tatooed, but Raven said it was a birthmark. That it connected her to the place of her origin, in the northeast.

"So, we saw." Raven said now. "What did we see?"

"We saw the bomb," Allie said, simply.

"I know we saw the bomb," Raven grinned. "But what did we 'see?' "

"I dunno what *you* saw," Allie said. "You have to tell me."

"Well, aside from the obvious, I saw my hand-bones. That was definitely strange. And I felt, rather than saw, what it must be like to become a wave of light. I was carried up by the blast and the sight of it, carried entirely out of myself, in an odd way I can't describe, except to say it was a physical sensation. Like a horse had kicked me and I was flying through the air."

"Did you hear anything or see anything else while you were there?"

"No, not really. Only like being whited out, blazed out. I dunno. I can't really get the words around it."

"I've seen a lot of these," Allie said, "and I still don't get exactly what they're about. I mean, I know they're about war, but that's not the important part. I don't mean war's unimportant," she grinned, "but there's more to it than just destruction, at least I think there is. I mean, nothing's only destruction. What destroys also creates, especially something like this. So what's it creating? What's being created?"

"The white man doesn't create. He destroys."

"Oh, don't go political on me, Eddie Raven."

"That's not politics, Allie Hawker. It's history."

"Yeah, I know, but lookit here. Even the history of our people and the whites isn't just destruction, is it?"

"Certainly not. The whites are doing just fine." Raven looked down at her fine leather boots. "I guess some of us are doing all right, too," she added in a low voice.

"Yeah, all these goodies and trinkets," Allie grinned and lifted her binoculars to the sky. "How'd we ever do without them!"

"Gracefully, that's how," Raven said sarcasm marbling her remark like fat in prime-grade steak.

"Well," Allie said, "let's go get breakfast. We don't have to figure the whole thing out right this minute."

They turned and began the descent from the peak. As they were walking along the dim trail, Raven realized Allie hadn't told her what she had seen. She also remembered something else she, Raven had seen, but had nearly forgotten in her amazement at the whiteness of the light, how it had seemed to flatten, to drain all color and form from her mind as well as from her range of vision. She was filled once again with it, the amazement, the blinding, flattening, stunning brightness of the white storm that had lifted her from herself. "An old woman," she said, her voice sharp with excitement. "I remember now. I saw an old woman's face, somewhere. Maybe in the cloud." She felt confusion as she realized that location was not the same in the mind place she had been catapulted to as in the physical world. 'In the blast' didn't mean the same on the plain as in her thought, her mind's picture of it. "Like in the blast, but not the one out there, the one in here," she gestured excitedly at her head.

Allie looked over her shoulder at Raven, not breaking her stride. "What did she look like, can you say?"

"Like the light. Like a great white bear that grew and grew and filled everything. Like an old woman." Raven shook her head rapidly back and forth to clear it. "I can't say it," she said, laughing helplessly at her stumbling language, its inadequacy. At the stubborn materiality of them in the face of what was not even remotely like the material, the physical they suggested. She was taken aback to hear her companion's shout of glee.

"I knew it!" Allie exclaimed, jumping a foot into the air in her excitement. "I knew it! Old woman! I knew it!" She whirled to grab Raven by the elbows and catch her up in her jumping up and down, emitting the high, piercing trill of the women as she did so. "I knew you had to come with me, that somehow you are connected to all this! I just knew it!" she shouted. And dropping her arms from her lover's elbows, she whirled again and began leaping and running down the path, trilling lustily as she ran.

"Boy," thought Raven watching her usually broody lover race madly down the path, "if she likes that, she'll love the part about my birthmark!" She walked unhurriedly along the path Allie had so precipitously negotiated, lighting a cigarette to keep her company as she ambled along enjoying the normal soft brilliance of the desert winter sun, remembering the sight of the birthmark in the unearthly light that illumined interiors through closed eyes.

When she had put her hand before her eyes and seen the bones, she had also seen the birthmark, glowing with a certain light that made it pulsate. It had gone from its usual shade of dull dark bronze to brilliant gold, then to a dazzling orange, then to a red that she could not begin to describe. She had never seen colors like those, nor like the rest of the hues it had turned, moving along the spectrum from the red to violet, to a kind of blue that most closely resembled a gas flame, but infinitely more radiant. It seemed to emit the colors rather than to reflect them, she mused. Like it was making them somehow, not like they colored it. She knew she would never be able to convey in words what she had seen, no more than what she had felt in the time she had watched the strawberry mark undergoing its luminous, radiant transformations. At the height of intensity it had begun to spin, too fast to keep track of, really, and had gone from ultra-blue to a brilliance she could only call white, though she knew that was not the name of it.

And as it was spinning it seemed to emit a sound or a tone that was beyond her range of hearing, but which she knew was sound. That was when she had seen the old woman or great white bear or sun maiden or sun shield, she now recalled. In her memory's eye she could see that the visual was of an old woman's face, huge as the sky, but that in some way that was not visual she had identified it as sun, bear, and shield—not in sequence with each other, but simultaneously. As if it was sunbearshield and it, they, took on the face of old woman as their shape.

As she pondered the fluid image, she felt something happen in her head, as though a curtain blew open for a moment, as though something wrenched the usual pool of thought and feeling that she identified as herself, and beside, behind it, she glimpsed, only for a split second, a low-ceilinged rectangular room, had the impression of four ancient crones and a very young girl, four small fires blazing . . . then it was gone. She felt dizzy, nauseated. "What was that?" she exclaimed aloud. And stood stock still trying to recover the impression. A longhouse, something. . . .

After a few minutes of intense effort, she gave up the attempt as futile. Shrugging philosophically, she put her hands in her pockets and continued her walk back to camp. She made an effort to put her thoughts into order, and after a few brisk strides she succeeded. One of the good things about being hungry is it takes your mind off impossible things, she thought. I wonder if Allie's got the coffee brewing. Cheered by the thought, she quickened her pace, already imagining the taste of rich coffee on her tongue, the smell of cedar from the fire fragrant on the morning air. She felt surrounded by some kind of presence, by some kind of presence, and she relaxed into it, letting the peace of the morning enter her, making her again complete.

"Good god," she sighed, "I love being free."

Chapter 2

In the deepening light of late afternoon, Allie turned her car west on the freeway, sighing with relief. She had dropped her friends off uptown, and now she was alone, on her way home. She loved the light as it was now, transforming the bleak mesas and the dusty city into a blazing effulgence of radiance. The shadows on the west mesa were long and deep, and the trees that filled the valley and lined the river at the lowest point of it threw gold into the air, a gold that was met by the gold of the dying sun. There were thunderheads piled tall and brooding on the edges of the world, mumbling their incantations deep in their ripening bellies. An occasional flash of lightning darted from their purple sides, testing its power along the clay and sandstone of the ground. She was filled with the fierce exultation that always came over her when she swooped down from the heights of the east or west mesa, speeding toward the valley floor; from light into shadow she plummeted, falling into the purple and green of the bosque's welcoming embrace. At the Rio Grande exit she left the freeway and turned north, feeling the simple excitement she always felt at this turn, the anticipation, as her mind, her spirit, flew ahead of her, darting and dipping through the cottonwoods along the twisting curves of the west valley roads she drove steadily toward home. "Eagle am I," she chanted quietly, her voice deep and rumbling in her chest. "An eagle I fly."

It was her own song, one she had gotten from an eagle, that an eagle had given her. She had been out camping in the mountains of Washington, had spent weeks out there in the wilds, alone and half wild herself. That was long ago; years. Before she had become what she was, while she was still becoming. She was in her twenties then, fresh out of the service. "I'm a free woman," she would say, laughing with sardonic humor at the absurdity of the statement. Even then she knew the difference between discharged and free. She knew that no one got discharged from America.

But for those weeks in the hills, alone with herself and whatever creatures chose to speak with her, alone with the great waters, the vast skies, the incurable rain, the endless forests, she knew freedom. And when she spoke of it, she knew what she was saying.

She had joined the army young, because she had heard a strange thing, because she was restless and full of angry vitality, because it was better than reform school, her alternative option. She had finished school, if that was what that miserable place could be called, and drunk with independence had returned home, where she learned another kind of drunkenness.

Her parents were dead by then, dead of the despair that afflicted so many of the People, and she didn't miss them any more dead than she had alive. They had been lost to her long before their deaths.

Sent to boarding school when she was very small, abducted more than sent, actually, by white government agents as so many were during the years between the last of the Indian wars and the Second World War, her life had been confined to institutional care, uncare, most of the time. She hardly remembered her parents, hardly knew them. She had spent some summers with them, just a few. The white powers felt that it was best for the children to stay away from the Indian community as much as possible. If they had had their way, no Indian child would have returned home after they were stolen and placed in the jail for children, the concentration camp for infant prisoners of war, until each had been so thoroughly brainwashed, whitewashed, that there would be no Indian spirit or mind left in that Indian body. Where they had not suffered much more than gross neglect, laced more or less sparingly with abuse, and liberally dosed with daily, hourly, fear and humiliation. Not much more than that, but it would do.

A few had died of grief, starvation, beatings, running away, food poisoning, infections that went untreated; still, most had survived. Bitter with helplessness to be sure, but alive, they went out into the great world to find their fortune and make their way. The mutilation of spirit that they had undergone did not show, not in any obvious way. It was a peculiar mutilation, mutation, one that ensured that, for the most part, they would become the kind of Indian white propaganda had determined was the only kind there was: savage, impoverished, broken, and hostile, abjectly in need of the white man's salvation, his mercy, his compassion, his friendship, his regard—which, they had been thoroughly, painstakingly trained to know, they could never really gain.

After her "graduation," as they called it—it simply meant they judged her sufficiently tamed to be let loose—on the longer tether they named reservation lands, equipped with her BIA card so she could be tracked wherever she might roam in that land of the free, that home of the braves who were dead and dying still, she had made her way back to Coyote, a tiny village in Oklahoma, where she moved in with her grandmother, grandfather, and assorted relatives.

Avid for excitement, she had started running with a fast crowd, had left the village for Oklahoma City, where she hit the streets for a time, "stolen by deer woman," they used to say, and was arrested for prostitution. In jail she had made a few friends, several enemies, and when she had finally been hauled before the justice of the peace—a weasle-like little man who had food or something worse stuck disgustingly in his mustache—and he gave her a choice between the army and the penitentiary, or reform school if it turned out she insisted on proving that she was under age, she chose the army. At least there, she reasoned, she would get paid. She could still party, drink and dance, and raise hell. As for the danger—it was not part of her experience to worry about it. Danger and life were, to her, part and parcel of the same thing. "You get what you pay for," she would say, and "I'm too broke to pay for much."

But what really decided her was something she had heard. She had been at a stomp dance in some Choctaw village, and late in the night she had taken her blanket to a place near some trees, away from the dance grounds. She had spread it out and lain down, prepared to sleep. But she could hear some women talking, low, somewhere near, so she got up to investigate. They heard her coming, and called out to her to join them, and she did. Then they went back to their conversation. She couldn't see their features clearly in the dark, but she knew they were pretty old from their voices and the way they held themselves, so still, so quiet. They were talking about a strange thing that was coming, one of them had seen it when she had been out praying in the hills, the low, leafy mountains of eastern Oklahoma and Arkansas. There were long pauses between the sentences they exchanged.

"I'm not sure what it was," one was saying. "It looked like the ground opened up and the thunders emerged. The sky cracked open as well. There was light, oh, the light, climbing and climbing toward the heavens. It had been dark, as I was just walking around and singing, you know." The other nodded. Allie nodded too, though she wasn't sure if she knew what the woman meant.

"There was so much light," she repeated, gesturing sharply with her right hand as though poking the darkness in front of her with a stick. She was silent for a long time. As she waited, Allie did not wonder if she would say more. She knew the women might not. Women as old as these had the old ways, and did not say so much aloud as younger ones did.

But she was content to sit, to listen to the insects' song counterpoint the turtle-shell music of the dancers and their singing. She was comfortable there in the warm, welcoming dark, watching the flickers cast into the night by the fires that ringed the dance ground.

After a long silence, the old woman spoke again. "I think they have opened the earth. Earth woman is being made to bring something forth. I think they do not know this, but my vision tells me it's so. Maybe they are preparing her for our new life. But many will try and stop the birth. We must watch, and wait. Maybe there will be some way to make sure her time comes as it should."

They said no more and after an hour or more Allie felt herself drifting off to sleep. She rose quietly and returned to her blanket, rolled herself up in it, and slept.

But when the dirty little justice of the peace said he would sign the papers saying she was old enough to enlist in the army, she remembered the woman's words. Something in her leaped with joy as he spoke; something said, "Go to the white man's war. You will learn what is needful there."

And so she went. And by another odd twist of circumstance, she was in New Mexico on leave the summer of 1945, had driven down to the southern mountains with some friends where they camped out in the mountains near Alamogordo. And there they witnessed the truth of the old woman's tale. "Oh, the light, the light," that old woman had said, and in her memory Allie saluted her, repeating, "so much light, oh, the light." Yes, that was why she had joined the army; so she could witness the birth of Sun woman.

"An eagle am I." She needed the song often. She spent so

much time with heterosexual women, so much energy protecting herself from discovery. The eagle had given her the song as a protection and a reminder that freedom was a lonely and bloodthirsty affair. It had come to her, sailing in the high sky over the peaks that towered above her small camp after several days during which she had been seeking and praying. She had been seeking an answer; praying for a sign—a vision, maybe; a dream; a talking stick—whatever the supernaturals might send her way in answer to her voice, calling them. And the song was not all of what they sent. No, they had been generous, that she knew; and also that their generosity would exact its own terrible price before the doing was done. Still, she had been grateful. Not softly so, of course; softness was not her way. But what she had seen let her know her place in the dance of things, and made a circumstance that could have been bitter had she gone in that direction with it instead a source of strong pride and determination. Vindication, maybe; certainly hot-blooded fierceness of joy. "An eagle am I," now she chanted, shouting. Letting go of the steering wheel momentarily. Reaching her arms over and behind her head. Stretching herself as the eagle had stretched herself, singing. Feeling the speed of flight as the car sped homeward in the gathering dark, arms stretching into the dusk behind her head. Then returning them to the wheel, she laughed, "and queer as hell."

from *The Sharpest Sight*

Louis Owens

The arrows of death fly unseen at noon-day;
the sharpest sight can't discern them.

Jonathan Edwards
*Sinners in the Hands
of an Angry God*

Cole McCurtain

In the fall, when red and gold leaves lay on the sand and the sycamores stood like cold shadows, when the rains of the last winter
had been forgotten and the new rains hadn't come yet and the
river was only a feeling beneath the clean sand of its bed, when
the brush had receded to clumps and mats of tangled black and
gray between the islands of trees, then the hunters would appear
in the early mornings tracking the frost and breathing puffs of

smoke. With sharp movements of winter the rabbits would dart like small fists from clumps of brush to race across the sand and leaves and disappear into identical clumps, the brush rabbits like dark spasms and the larger cottontails heavy and quivering with life. On those fall days the sky would have climbed higher, lifted on the drop of the leaves and the swift rise of the smooth trunks. Sounds would snap in the cold air like thin branches. On those days I would pull on the old wool pants, flannel shirt, fatigue jacket with the words on it, lugsoled boots, and fingerless gloves and leave the house by the back door, reaching the riverbank in a dozen long strides and plunging to the sand six feet below, the worn barrel of the .22 glinting dully like the frost on the dead grass. No longer was it a balancing of desire and reflexes against the small life of the riverbottom. It had become a ritual, like counting the hawks that flew up when you drove the country roads.

My father is a half-breed. That makes me a quarter-breed. Actually a three-eighths breed, since my mother is a quarter Cherokee like just about everybody else who ever lived in Oklahoma. Well, the fact is she's really three-eighths Cherokee, since her mother was three-quarters and born in the Nation and had *my* mother when she was thirteen and not even five feet tall. So I guess that makes me a seven-sixteenths breed—almost a half-breed like my father. Let's say I'm nearly a half-breed, whatever that means. My father knows, but what I know from books in school and the old movies on television is that a half-breed can't be trusted, is a killer, a betrayer, a breed.

My father is Choctaw. Hoey McCurtain is his name, and there were chiefs in his family, or so he says when he's had a few beers. Personally, I think it's just as likely they were bonepickers, growing their fingernails long for their task down there in Mississippi where I remember air like water and water like earth. Cole McCurtain is my name, and I fish the subterranean Salinas River. We Indians have always lived close to the land, my father says, Mother Earth, turtle's back. He's shorter than me, only five-eight, and broad through the shoulders and dark, with burnt-rust skin, black hair, and black eyes (except for the milky one where the carburetor exploded in his face). I'm taller, five-ten, thinner, lighter—from the Cherokee and Irish, I guess. An almost half-breed with green slanty eyes who fishes the quiet water that runs underground. As my older brother Attis used to say when he was alive, it's hard as hell to tell who you are in this family. Only thing for sure, he'd say, is there's some nuts blood somewhere in the ancestry. Attis would have understood what happened after he died—about Diana and Blake, maybe even about Landra and the soulcatcher—would have shrugged the way he always did, his broad, dark face and black eyes accepting it all. But there were some things I had to learn about Attis, too.

The Salinas is a sand-and-brush-and-cottonwood river with clean-limbed sycamores along the banks. And down below the white sand the river runs in a strong current. You can feel it thrumming there beneath your feet when you fish it, hear the current sliding along down there, almost see the fish that fin in the invisible water. It's the largest subterranean river in the world, they say, and in the late winter and early spring, when the rains come hard, it rises out of the ground and becomes a real river, a half-mile-wide stretch of brown water that drags away trees and topsoil and bathtubs and chicken coops with chickens all over them and now and then a bridge. Like *oka falama,* Hoey McCurtain says, the Choctaw version of the big flood. Then, after a week or so it starts to disappear, sinking back into the sand so that only pools are left here and there, with a little clear stream at the heart of the sand. And when the pools dry up you see coon tracks pressed into the sand around the tails and bones of big fish. And then even the little stream sinks down below the sand and the Salinas becomes an underground river again. That's when I fish it.

Sometimes I hunt down there, too, sending the fat little cottontails or brush rabbits tumbling into limp fluffs with my brother's .22. Indians have always been hunters, my father says, often. He's a hunter, would hunt the last animal on earth, I think, track it down and kill it and then look around in real surprise at what the world had come to. It's deep in the blood. The Salinas, great underground sand river, is a long way from the Yazoo swamps where he grew up hunting coons and possums and alligators, but we make the most of it. It's not the same kind of river as the dark, deep Yazoo, where I remember the shadows rising and turning in the thick water, and I'm the only one who fishes it. A displaced Choctaw-Cherokee California subterranean fisherman whose monofilament sweeps in an endless arc, lost in the unbelievably clear water that no one sees.

In the fall, the sycamore and cottonwood leaves cover the cold sand and the river is between rains, the brush black between the trees. That's the time for hunting, after the rabbits are all big enough to get around by themselves and when the danger of valley fever is over. It was still gray, with the sycamore branches black against Pine Mountain when I came out that morning—the day it all sort of came together. Behind me I felt something like a groan, and when I turned the sun was resting on the top of Pine Mountain, three miles away, sending thin splinters of light down through the digger pines and oaks and probably the stones of the old graveyard, though I couldn't see that far.

I hadn't taken five steps from the porch when Zeke, the spaniel-mix rabbit dog that used to belong to Attis, was awake and scuttering down toward the river, his orange back just a flash when he went past. A good dog, but too fast for a rabbit dog. A good rabbit dog shouldn't get too close to the rabbit, but Zeke damned near caught them every time, so that often as not they would light out for the next county instead of making a circle like they're supposed to. You can't train a dog not to be too fast, Attis said. You can't train a brother not to be too stupid, I thought, watching the red brush of Zeke's tail vanish over the bank. Or too foolish.

"Yea though I walk through the valley of the shadow of death" in magic marker on the back of the jacket, blocky letters the way a kid would write it. He'd sent me the jacket back early, along with the only letter he'd ever written me, since his second hitch was almost up. "I shall fear no evil, for I am. . . ." Can't tell who the hell what the hell you are with the sand hidden under the red and orange leaves the water sweeping rushing along down there so clean and cold. The rabbits stir the leaves when they run, breaking from one black clump of brush to thrash across the leaves and disappear into an identical clump unless I use the .22. The sky climbs high on fall mornings, and that morning the crunch of leaves and small limbs was sharp on the air, like breaking bird-wings. The frost was silver on the dead stalks of wild oats, and I wasn't sure why I was out there.

"For I am the meanest motherfucker in the valley." They never opened it, just put a flag over it and stuck it in Pine Mountain, up there where the sun was hung up like blood now in the clumsy digger pines. For a moment, with a feeling like hatred, I watched the black points of the pines where they penetrated the reddening light, and then a second feeling came down the mountain with the sunlight, a strange kind of jealousy for something I couldn't name.

When Zeke flushed the first rabbit I was thinking of the Mekong Delta, and when he yapped out of sight after the cottontail I just watched the two of them throw up leaves and cross the bare patches of sand till they disappeared into another island of cottonwoods and brush.

I waited, listening to a flicker knocking against a dead tree close by, sounding as if he was going to take the whole thing down, the hammering nailing me to the cold morning. I started to think of Diana, and that made me think of Landra, since I couldn't think of one without the other, and then Blake and Hiawatha weaseled into the picture. Using a trick Attis had taught me, I shoved them all into a black tunnel at the back of my mind and rolled a big rock into the mouth of the cave. The bare patch of sand I stood on was hard with frost and I could feel the vibration of the river coming through my legs. The gun was cold on my fingers and I shifted it to my left hand so I could wedge my right hand under my left armpit. In a few seconds the feeling came back and so did the rabbit.

A cottontail, its big white ass held high, the rabbit crawled out of a cluster of brush twenty feet away, crawling kind of like a cat, the way people who haven't seen them will never believe they crawl. Then it sat back on its fat haunches and sniffed the cold air, waiting for me to put a small round chunk of lead through it. The brown fur was sleek and the ears twitched a little while the nose worked, but I was upbreeze so he couldn't smell anything except Zeke, wherever Zeke was.

I lifted the old rifle, so worn that the sun was shining in a line along the barrel, and lined up the notch sight on a spot just below the ear facing me and pulled back the hammer and shouted.

At the shout, the cottontail leaped and spun and vanished into the brush it had appeared from, and then I saw Zeke sitting fifty feet further up the stretch of sand, watching me. Then my father spoke and I flinched.

"You're going to ruin that dog."

He was standing a few feet away when I turned, his hands in the pocket of the old red-plaid wool coat, the collar turned up around his thick neck so that the face was framed between black collar and black John Deere baseball cap.

"You go letting a dog down that way too often, you're going to break his spirit, even a old turdeater like that." He spat a stream of tobacco juice onto the pattern of leaves and shook his head.

"How come you don't shoot?" His voice sounded skeptical. The one dark eye was keen, and as I started to answer, I felt Zeke's cold nose against my hand where the rifle dangled at my side. I swung the long barrel of the gun away from my father's groin, uncocked it, and pushed the safety on. I was usually careful about the safety when I hunted. He had shifted his head a little to one side when I turned back—to take better advantage of the good eye. My father's the only person I know who would pour gasoline in a carburetor to get a motor started and then look to see if the carburetor was flooded so that it would blow up right in his face. Not that he's stupid. Hoey McCurtain's one of the smartest men I've ever seen in some ways.

I didn't know how to explain because it was the first time I'd realized I didn't shoot anymore, that I hadn't shot for a long time. I tried to think back to a time when I had hunted for something more real than whatever it was that I'd come to be hunting for now, and my memory ran up against the wall of Attis's funeral seven months before and around the edge of that memory was the shadow, that thing down there in the river that I wasn't ready to put a name to yet, though I knew the name.

"Time flies when you're having a good time," our mother used to say when Attis and I were kids and thought it was too early to come in from whatever it was we were doing—playing stretch with our pocketknives or knocking little birds out of trees with our bb guns.

"What's the matter, your tongue froze up?" He shifted the lump in his cheek, and I remembered the way he used to talk to Attis.

A red-tailed hawk settled on a cottonwood a few hundred yards downstream. The sun had torn itself free of Pine Mountain now and was looking down on us, and I saw that my father's hair was getting longer these days, past his ears and over the edges of his collar. Maybe he was going to start braiding it, though I didn't think Choctaws braided their hair from the pictures I'd seen. I thought about asking him. He would know. He was getting more and more Indian everyday, and the more Indian he got the crazier he seemed to me, like he was trying to make himself into something I couldn't even imagine, something as impossible to me as the Mississippi swamp he used to disappear into every night.

Lately he'd been doing more reading and complaining about what a bastard Thomas Jefferson had been. For a long time he was always after Andy Jackson, a red-necked sonofabitch in my father's words, but recently he'd taken to throwing in Jefferson, claiming that Jefferson had thought up the use of trading posts as a way to get Indian land without shooting Indians, just get them in debt and take the land in payment. Now Jefferson was a phony blue-blood sonofabitch. "The father of our country, hah!" he'd snort, maybe confusing Jefferson with Washington, I thought. Since he'd taken up reading about it, he was getting more and more sore about what a raw deal the Choctaw had gotten in Mississippi. Before it got too cold, Mundo Morales used to come over and the two of them would sit out back drinking Blue Ribbon and complaining about what a raw deal their folks had got, Mundo bitching about how Morales used to own the whole god-damned county and Hoey McCurtain topping that with how the Choctaw used to own all Mississippi and part of Louisiana. With their black hair and skin the color of old blood, they looked quite a bit alike. The difference was that Mundo was the law and Hoey McCurtain the outlaw.

"Indians don't yell 'bang' when they go after meat," he said, hunching his shoulders.

I shrugged. "Maybe it was the Irish," I said, thinking that after all I was more Irish than anything else, one-sixteenth more. Then I got back to wishing I could feel like something the way Mundo Morales and Hoey McCurtain did, Indian or Irish or something. You are what you think you are, he'd once told me. He thought he was Choctaw, not just Indian but Choctaw.

"Irish my ass," he said. "Come on, let's get some breakfast before we get at that fence."

I nodded and reached down to scratch Zeke's spaniel ear, feeling like I'd let the dog down—Attis's dog—and surprised to realize that I had been hunting without shooting for a long time without knowing it, or without thinking about it, which amounts to the same thing, I guess. I couldn't feel the river any longer as I followed my father back toward the gray house.

In the kitchen, my mother was frying venison and eggs, splashing the grease up over the eggs to make the edges lacy and brown. Her dark hair wisped out in strands from the bun she'd twisted it into, the Oklahoma Cherokee blood obvious in the fine edges of her cheekbones and the black pupils of her narrow eyes. She looked tired, more tired than it seemed a person could be, and I wondered how a woman with only one husband and two kids could get that way. Maybe from being married for twenty years to Hoey McCurtain, a California Choctaw living in a made-up world who was busy creating himself out of books and made-up memories so that it was plain he was leaving the rest of us behind. As if you could really choose what you were going to be instead of just being what it was you had to be.

"Coffee's in the thermos," she said. "Your lunches are on the table."

She slid two of the creamy brown eggs onto a plate and forked a piece of meat next to them and then repeated the action for my father. He'd taken off the heavy coat and stood in the kitchen doorway, scratching the belly that was beginning to show over his trucker's buckle. He carried his plate to the table and came back for a loaf of bread.

I picked up the plate and said "Thank you," and she smiled and reached out to put a hand on my shoulder, a gesture it seemed one of us was always making, like practicing for one day when we'd be affectionate or something. Then she turned back toward the stove, one of those old stoves that had gas burners but looked like a woodburner. It was probably an antique, I thought.

"That old stove's probably worth some money," I said. To make her feel better, I guess, about not having an up-to-date stove like everyone else.

She smiled again and said, "Your eggs are getting cold."

As I carried my plate to the table in the other room, I wondered what kind of stove Diana's mother had.

After breakfast, we drove through Amarga out toward the fence we were building in the hills near Morro Bay. Amarga was wide awake, with all those ranchers and grain farmers coming in early to get first crack at the hardware store and feed-supply and sit around coffee at Hong's Cafe and talk about hard lives. The town isn't much, with its crummy bowling alley, supermarket, half-a-dozen bareass stores of one kind or another and the same number of bars. Even after ten years, it wasn't a town I could feel much about one way or another, except to respect the casual violence that lay close to the surface of every town like that.

Behind the dirty window of the County Sheriff's substation, Mundo Morales was fooling around with his coffee pot. Pretty soon, I knew, he'd have to lock up his gun and badge and go clean toilets at the high school up the hill. Being a custodian up there was his real job, and being the town's only deputy sheriff, and a part-time one at that, was what he did for fun. And he got his share of fun in Amarga. Like the time the guys in the Letterman's Club threatened to execute a whole rooters' bus from Paso Robles, or the time Daryl Lance dug up his grandma. Both of those things had happened last year, when I was still in school.

The narrow road snaking over the coast range was empty except for the Dodge pickup we rattled along in, and I looked down at the live-oak-and-brush-choked creek a hundred feet below the road and remembered the black trout we used to catch there. Squirming through the tunnel of creek brush to drift a worm into the dark ripples below the little falls, me and Attis taking turns at each hole. The six-pound monofilament would drift unweighted from the cut-down fiberglass poles over the falls into the gently boiling small pools and then there would be a faint tug and a shiver on the line that tingled all the way up your arm and you would pull a small dark tumult of shadow six or seven or eight inches long out of the black water. It was always cool and hidden down there, and we'd crawl and fish for miles down the creekbed where it fell toward the coast and know we were the only ones to ever fish the blackest pools.

Hoey McCurtain

It was colder than a bitch out there by the time we got to the place we were building the fence. I'd run a gold string along the fenceline where it climbed up the hill. Cole dragged the two-handled pipe we used as a post-pounder from where we'd stuck it under a tree, and we got back at it, pounding those red poles into the shaley ground.

A couple of scrawny clouds were sitting on top of the coast range, and while I watched Cole hammering with that pipe, I could hear a car whining up the grade from Amarga. The way he worked, I could tell his mind was wandering around again, like a pup sniffing at gopher holes. That and the jacket he was wearing, the one that used to be Attis's, got me to thinking again about the differences between the two. Attis had been short and kind of dark like me, so that anybody could tell he was Indian right away, Choctaw if they knew what Choctaw looked like. But with Cole you couldn't really tell unless you looked close. I'd never said nothing to him, but it was likely he'd lose his hair when he got to be my age, he took so much after his mother's side where all the men had been bald as eggs by the time they were fifty, Cherokee blood or no Cherokee blood. Then I started thinking about the Nemi girl, who'd been Attis's girl before he went to Nam, and wondering about her and Cole. Sometimes I'd get to missing Attis so much it'd feel like I'd sprung a leak inside and was going to empty out, and then I'd try to think of something else. Now I got to considering that black girl, Landra Jones.

He finished with the post and set the pipe down, and I pulled at the post to see if it was in good. It gave a little and sprang back, and I looked at all the posts we'd already drove that morning.

"Let's take a break," I said, "before hitting those corner posts."

He nodded and kicked the driver out of the way, so that it was nearly hidden in the dead grass and I made a note of where it was so he wouldn't have to hunt all over hell for it later. Cole was a hell of a worker, but he was always doing things like that, not thinking ahead.

We both sat down near the thermos Ida had sent, and while he opened it I admired the fence we were building for Dougherty. Under the trees, the leaves and oats were still all gray with frost.

Cole poured coffee into the mug with the crack up the side and handed it to me, saving the thermos cup for himself.

"Sleepy?" I asked. He was looking down into that plastic cup, the way some people look when they're reading a book, all hunched up like he was cold, even though it wasn't that cold anymore.

"I was thinking about when we used to go deer hunting out near Creston," he said.

"I went out there in August," I answered, adding, "I asked you to come."

"I was thinking about before," he said.

I noticed that the sun was finally up over the ridge, but kind of dull and washed out. "Attis is dead," I said. "It don't do no good to keep thinking about it."

I heard another car—no, a truck this time—grinding up the road toward the pass below us. "What are you going to do about the draft?" I asked, figuring I might as well get that out in the open. "They'll come and get you like they did that Jorgenson boy."

Ricky Jorgenson had been Cole's friend when they were kids. Jorgenson had volunteered for the Marines and then went AWOL, hiding with his old lady at home till they come and took him.

He'd left his legs in a field somewhere in Vietnam and was up there on the hill with Attis.

"You don't owe this sonofabitchin' government anything," I said.

He got up and pulled on one of his gloves and then took it off and emptied out the little rocks that always get down into the fingers. "I remember what you told Attis," he said; then he went over to the railroad ties we'd brought up for corner posts and started to move them around like he was looking for something—snakes probably, though it was too late in the year and too high and cold for snakes.

"You don't owe the bastards nothing," I said. "They made Pushmataha a brigadier general, a goddamned general, him thinking that now it would be okay, now they'd get to stay in Mississippi. They gave him a gold medal in Washington after the Choctaws won the Battle of New Orleans for them. And then that red-neck sonofabitch Jackson sent in the troops to steal the land and cattle and slaves and everything else and move them all to Oklahoma, except it wasn't Oklahoma yet and he didn't know nothing about oil. My folks—your folks—didn't go. Hid out in the woods and starved and didn't end up with diddlysquat. Andy Jackson said fuck the Supreme Court and marched all them war heroes straight to Oklahoma. That's what you owe those bastards."

I hadn't meant to give him the lecture again, but it just came out, and I knew he wasn't even listening. He had both gloves on now and was carrying the posthole digger to the place for the corner posts. When he was little, he'd had rheumatic fever and had to stay in bed for three months. They'd said his heart wouldn't never be as strong as it was before that, but he'd outgrown it. I had to admit that not even Attis was a better worker.

"You were a paratrooper in the war." He had stopped with the posthole digger on his shoulder and was looking back at me.

He had me there. I said the only thing I could. "I was stupid, too young. I didn't know a goddamned thing."

He stuck the digger in the ground and levered up some loose dirt. I put the thermos back under the tree and carried the bar to where he was already working.

"What do you call that soulcatcher you told me about?" he asked suddenly. "That black thing?"

It took me a minute to shift gears, but then I remembered, "Souleater, you mean. The Choctaw call it *nalusachito*. Why?"

"Just curious." He jabbed the digger into the hole and didn't get anywhere, so I started in with the bar, breaking it up, trying to remember when I'd told him about the souleater, what some called soulcatcher.

from *A Report of the Proceedings*

Elizabeth Cook-Lynn

(These are excerpts from a novel-in-progress which uses an actual trial transcript as a part of the basis for plot. The setting is Northern Plains, the time is 1950–60. The characters are not actual persons and any resemblance to persons living or dead is purely accidental.)

They walked into the large room. There were many beds and all of them were filled with the smallest wraith-like bodies that John had ever seen. He was glad that Benno had never come to a place like this.

He felt her move toward the nearest bed.

"Tunkashila," she shouted into the bony, hollow face of the old man.

"How are you?"

There was no answer.

"Are you OK, grampa?"

"Toniktuka he?" She waited this time for him to look at her.

Hoarsely, the old man repeated the question that she'd just asked. "Toniktuka he?" he asked, bewildered. He looked at her searchingly, his dark eyes clouded, the pupils empty. John B, standing beside her, thought for an awful moment that she would start to weep.

"Toniktuka he?" the old man whispered pitifully.

Then he felt around the bed for his cane, moving the bed clothes this way and that until she took hold of his wrist and held his arm. With just a little pressure she got him to lie back and then she started to talk as though everything was all right:

"Grampa, I dug some wild turnips with that stick you made for me. Do you remember? I hung them over the stove to dry."

She lifted up his head and put a huge pillow under his thin neck.

"Here's one of them, grampa. One of them turnips. Here."
She put one in his mouth.

"They're pretty dry, grandpa," she hollered, "Just suck on it."

Then she put one in her own mouth and chomped hard on it.

"It got dark," she told him conspiratorially, "and the coyotes had to leave me on my own."

"Do you remember that, LaLa?" she smiled, and continued to talk, sharing with him secrets of the past.

John B had sat in the big leather chair beside the old man's bed that day and, even though he knew that the old man would be angry to see him there, he had stayed, compelled somehow to be with her as she made her duty-visit to the old grandfather.

He loved listening to her talk and even when she was drunk and behaving badly as she did sometimes, he was always reassured by just the mere sound of her voice. He noticed that she had the ability to adapt to the rhythm of a language and even to use the rhythm of one language to change the sound of another . . . and . . . so . . . when she talked in English she often used the sounds of Dakotah, the cadence and the tone of Dakotah speech.

What it amounted to, in John's mind, was a kind of purity of speech, a kind of attempt on her part to retain some of the sense of Dakotah aesthetic in everyday life. And it always reassured John in ways that he could not explain. Now he sat and listened to her work her spell on the old grandfather. And he thought how pleased the old man must be.

That morning she had talked to John B in much the same way while she sat on the edge of the bed at her place. John had covered his eyes with his arm, pretending to be unmoved by her.

What she had talked about that morning had made a deep impression on John, though, and as a result of her words he had decided that he would fire the lawyer who had been attempting his defense.

She had said:

> You know, John, the grass wisp dance was once disclaimed by my mother and the people of her tribe. Yes, I know, he had answered. She continued: they said to take off their clothes and paint themselves was evil. He had listened in silence to this story of hers, not really attentive to the subject matter because he had heard her tell it many times. She went on: they said that to pray to the East, West, North, and South (she motioned with her hands) was to pray to the winds. And it was, therefore, evil. And my mother came to believe that. Yes.

Impulsively, he had touched her thigh and she looked at him, startled. Then she smiled.

"A-aye-e-e-e," she scoffed, pushing his hand away. "You're always *doing* that." She'd made him move over and then she had stretched full length beside him. Her body was warm and soft and the story she had started to tell was momentarily forgotten.

After their lovemaking, John lay for a long time beside her knowing explicitly what Aurelia was alluding to in her discussion of her mother's response to new religious thought and practice in Indian Country. And he knew, too, that firing the lawyer would probably do no good.

The Trial: DAY ONE

Q. Well, now, do you know whether or not you sold any cattle from the first of that year (1966) up until the time that this count was made?

A.   Well, I sold some cattle last year.

Q.   Last year?

A.   Yes.

Q.   Was it before or after this count done by Will Bent of Pierre Credit in 1966?

A.   It was after.

Q.   I see. Well, did you sell any cattle before the count was taken? In other words, from January 1st of 1966 to this April date when you made the count?

MR. HANSEN: Again, your honor, I'm going to object to these leading questions.

THE COURT: Well, let's remember first of all, this witness is as he says, an Indian. He is halting. I'm not entirely sure how readily he understands the language. I'm not placing him as a reluctant or a hostile witness, but I think we do have to consider his education, his background; and I am going to rule out questions that suggest the answer but I am going to permit the United States attorney to ask questions that may be somewhat leading. Overruled. Now. Would you read the question again, please.

REPORTER: Did you sell any cattle before the count was taken? In other words, from January 1st of 1966 to this April date when you made the count?

A.   Yes.

Q.   When was that?

A.   Well, that was sometime during the fall; latter part of the summer or early fall.

Q.   Well, what year would that have been?

A.   That would be last year.

Q. The latter part of the summer or early fall of last year. Is that right?

A. Yes.

Q. Well, Mr. Tatekeya, maybe you don't understand quite what I'm getting at. Now, last year was 1966. Is that right?

A. Well, last year is when I sold them cattle.

Q. OK, and you say that was in the summer or the fall?

A. That was in the fall, I'd say.

Q. In the fall. Well now, what I'm getting at, you said that you sold some cattle in the fall of 1964, is that right?

A. That's right.

Q. And that's the only bunch of cattle you sold in 1964. Is that correct?

A. That's right.

Q. And that's the only bunch of cattle you sold in 1964? Is that correct?

A. That's right.

Q. And you said, I believe, that you didn't sell any cattle during 1965. Is that right or wrong?

A. That's right.

Q. Now then, did you sell any cattle from the time that you had these missing cattle . . . that's in the fall of 1965 . . . up to the time that you made the count in April of last year?

MR. HANSEN: Just a moment, Mr. Tatekeya, Your honor, I would like to make a standing objection here.

THE COURT: You may have a standing objection. I call your attention to a United States case of Antelope vs. the United States, an 8th Circuit case, in which you have an Indian whose testimony is somewhat halting, who was a little difficult understanding all of these matters, and where it appears necessary to ask leading questions to get the material facts involved. Now, I'm not going to let the U.S. Attorney testify or put words in this man's mouth, but I think that he is somewhat confused on dates, and because of the fact that he is Indian, I am going to permit leading questions.

MR. HANSEN: Well, so that I will not . . .

THE COURT: (interrupting) You may have a standing objection to all such questions. Now, the minute it reaches the point where the DA is doing the testifying instead of the witness you call my attention to it, and I'll sustain your objection probably because I'm not going to let the DA testify or suggest the answer.

MR. HANSEN: Well, I believe that to be the case right now, your honor. That's why I made the objection.

THE COURT: I don't believe so. Let's hear the question again.

REPORTER: Now then, did you sell any cattle from the time that you had these missing cattle . . . that's in the fall of 1965 . . . up to the time that you made that count in April of last year?

THE COURT: He's simply asking whether or not he sold any cattle during that time. He isn't suggesting the answer. Overruled.

A. Yes, I sold some.

Q. When was that? When did you sell these cattle?

A. I sold these cattle last fall, and this fellow came out this spring to check them.

Q. Well, Mr. Tatekeya, last year was 1966. Is that a fact or isn't that a fact.

A. Yes, that is a fact.

Q. Now, is it correct that you say you sold cattle in the summer or the fall of last year, 1966, is that right?

A. Yes, that's right.

Q. Now, these missing cattle that you testified to earlier, that was in the fall of what year.

A. '65.

Q. All right. Now, from the fall of 1965, then go through the winter months of 1966, the first part of 1966 up to April of 1966. Did you sell any cattle during that period of time?

A. No.

Q. Fine. Now. All right. Now, Mr. Tatekeya, when you noticed missing cattle during the fall of 1965, do you know what kind of cattle you were missing?

A. I think so.

Q. What were they?

A. Herefords.

Q. Well now, well, I mean, what were they? Steers? Heifers? Calves?

A. Well, there was eight cows, eight calves, eight yearling steers and 18 yearlings and two year old heifers.

The lawyers hunched over their papers at this answer, scribbling hastily.

MR. HANSEN: Just a minute. Just a minute. I'm sorry. I didn't get all of that. Wait.

THE COURT: I didn't get it all, either. Let's hear that over again. Would you say that again, Please?

A. (Slowly) Eight cows, eight calves, eight yearling steers and eighteen yearlings and two year old heifers.

He was glad his wife had moved to town to live with their married daughter and he then had the opportunity to live by himself for the first time since their marriage twenty years ago. He was a tall man about fifty years old and this morning, still cool and bright, starting the kind of day that would eventually get so muggy his clothes would hang damply around him, he found himself waiting for a representative of the Federal Bureau of Investigation so that they could search together the wind-swept hills of South Dakota and Nebraska for his stolen cattle.

He stirred the beans boiling in a pot on the gas stove but his mind wasn't on the business at hand. He was lost in thought, absorbed in the precious moments like this one that he shared with no one. The heat from the stove in the small one-room house would have seemed unbearable had he felt his own presence. Instead, he seemed untouched and untouchable.

He spooned the thick bean soup into a bowl, turned off the stove, and sat at the bare table eating silently, methodically, taking great care in breaking the crackers and dipping them slowly in the hot, salty bean soup. When he was nearly finished he sugared his coffee and sat stirring it with quick, short strokes, holding the spoon palm-up.

Minutes passed and he sat stirring, mixing, cooling. Finally, he lifted the bowl of coffee to his lips and quietly drained it.

He stood up and reached for his hat just as he heard footsteps at the door.

He stepped quickly outside.

"Ho," he said, feigning a graciousness he did not feel and he shook hands with the young man whose red hair almost matched his flaming cheeks so recently burned by the August wind which never ceased to blow across these prairies this time of year.

"You ready, John B?," asked the young man.

"Yeah," he said, "I'm ready."

FBI men were nothing new to this reservation in recent years, yet this one with the red hair and flaming cheeks seemed new and innocent and, somehow, frail. John B walked beside him to the government pickup truck, thinking silently about the incongruousness of them both, his own black, longish hair streaked with gray, the other man so pink and thin and freckled and young. A laughable, ridiculous pair, he mused.

Both were resolute, their common mission serious. They

okayed the horses, skitterish in the trailer hooked to the pickup. It was a long, hot trip to the rolling hills around Ainsworth, Nebraska, and they wanted to hurry. They had a long search ahead of them.

As they pulled away from John B's place, the small house surrounded by a stand of ancient cottonwood trees, the large corral and a couple of outbuildings blazing in the morning light with Red Hair, unaccustomed to the rough, rutted reservation road, driving carefully and slowly, John B let his eyes scan the fence lines.

Angry that his loss of 45 head of cattle was now in the hands of this punk kid who imagined that he represented the federal government's commitment to protect Indians from the thieves who surround them, he tried to think that this trip was something more than a gesture of futility.

The wind had blown clumps of weeds into the barbed wire fences which held them there and more piled up. By late fall, the fences would be clogged with thistles so thick a jackrabbit could hardly get through. It became a metaphor, in John's imagination, for his own struggle. The wind knows how to do things in the lives of men, thought John B, and the Dakotahs have lived explaining to themselves the significance of this power.

"My mother came to believe that it was evil to pray to the winds."
He saw her hands motioning.

His mother, too, had been easily persuaded by the simplicity of Christian beliefs to give up the complicated and difficult worship of the Four Winds and he, himself, because he had been her favorite son, was also dissuaded from practicing the old ways.

The outdoor bonfire at the church on Christmas Eve, the sounds of "Silent Night" rising in the night air; John B standing first on one foot in the bitter snow and then on the other; then, entering the Church singing Christmas carols and holding candles which acolytes set ablaze as each communicant entered: It was a comfort. It was less time-consuming and easier on the physical self than any of the Indian religious practices John knew.

He thought of the ease with which they had been led to believe in the white man's religion, and as the pickup driven by Red
Hair made its way down the graveled road and out of the bend in
the river, he pulled his hat down over his eyes and feigned sleep.

> "Old Hunka of the people, your scarred breast grows soft and trans-
> lucent in blue-grey photos on the wall in oval frames, hidden under
> dust. A man to be remembered, your ancient tongue warms men of
> fewer years and lesser view. You tell of those who came, too busy
> fingering lives with paper to know what they can't know . . . THEY
> LIKED THE ORATORY BUT THOUGHT THE CASE WAS HOPELESS: GO HOME, OLD
> BENNO, IT LOSES SOMETHING IN TRANSLATION. DRINK THE WIND AND
> DARKEN SCRAPS OF MEAT AND BONE. STARS WON'T RISE IN DREAMS AGAIN . . .
> heads bent to clay-packed earth, we smoke Bull Durham for bark of
> cedar . . . but know . . . in council, talk's not cheap nor careless in
> its passing. The feast begins with your aftervision, ahead of its time.
> We speak of you in pre-poetic ritual."

In the late fall months, old Benno had sat with him in the
blind and, together, they waited for the geese to settle on the
glaring ice and eventually waddle ashore where he could pick
off two or three with his 12-gauge. Sometimes he sneaked up on a
couple of the bigger ones, grabbing each by a leg and trussing
it quickly with leather thongs he held between his teeth.

Quickly, he would pluck the soft feathers from the underbelly
and between the legs and stuff the plumes into a buckskin bag,
paying no attention to the loud squawking of the terrified birds.
The aging Benno, breathing hard from the exertion, would drop
the smooth, black stone into this buckskin bag and walk three
miles to his house situated on a hillside away from the river and
the wind, and he would carefully place the bag in an old brown
mahogany dresser with his clothing and other articles he used
in ceremony.

The aftervision of old Benno, the old orator and traditional
singer of the tribe who had been declared incompetent by the
U.S. government because he wouldn't cut his hair and lease his
land to white men, came into John B's thoughts with no warn-

ing these days. And now that the old man was dead John tried to believe that he could go on living as though the world and mankind had a chance of surviving.

It was a pretense that John B grew ever more tired of perpetuating. There was no one, now, to speak ceremoniously of the most sacred power and the wisdom possessed by men like Benno and, since this power was rarely inherited or explained or understood, John B knew that the loss of the old man and his influence was irreconcilable and profound.

He tried to make sense of why this aftervision of Benno was so much on his mind lately. He could not say why that was so and even after the trial and for the rest of his life, he continued to carry with him the ever-present memory of the old man. Perhaps it signaled some kind of change in John B as he grew older. Perhaps it was because the old man in every gesture, in every word, in every event, had restored the ethical nature of how a man might live if he appropriately isolated himself.

Whatever the reason, John B knew that this kind of ethical influence was reserved for certain others like Benno ... not for himself. But when he thought about how to survive, he began to wonder, facetiously at first, if he himself was going to have to become celibate as Benno had been in later life, giving up women and booze and the good times. Because religious ideas are always connected to the ethics of survival, John B continued to recall Benno's finding of the black stone, the prayers to the Four Winds, the gathering of the goose down. He continued to regret that it had become so difficult to find the stone, that such sacred religious symbols were not easily acquired during this time when life-styles had changed so drastically.

And in the end, he accepted the sorrow of the loss of this significant old man's companionship whose memory continued to be whispered by the prairie wind, not knowing what message for the future was possible.

Even though he did not speak the old man's name and never heard it on the lips of those around him, he knew that he was not alone in the belief that the old singer was the one who had seen the shadows moving near and had warned them.

The horses in the trailer grimly held their positions as the government rig pressed southward, Red Hair talking and chewing gum with equal vigor and John B silently musing about his own culpability concerning the theft which had cut his herd in half.

He had been drunk for days and was told later that he had been seen in Presho, Chamberlain, Pierre, even Sturgis and Rapid City. And now, here he was after four months, driving to Nebraska with this red-haired kid to see if he could identify his cattle which had been sold piecemeal at several regional sale barns. The four wires of the fence had been stretched and held to the ground, he knew now, and a large truck had been driven into the pasture, sidled up to the corral and loading chute, and 45 head of John B's herd of 107 horned Herefords had been loaded out. It had probably taken three or four men to do the job on a moonlit night and, silent and unnoticed, they had probably driven down this same isolated road.

Ruefully, John recalled the agony of his own behavior and he could think of no excuses. He had gotten back to the place nearly two weeks after the theft. He was nauseated, red-eyed, and aching from too much liquor and too many nights laid out in the back of his pickup.

He had gone from pasture to pasture, at first driving his pickup because he felt so sick; later, astride his old buckskin gelding. He had asked the neighbors for information and then had gone back to search the adjoining pastures again and again. He had walked the subirrigated eighty acres along the river but had seen no signs. And, then, he had gone back to the neighbors who merely shook their heads and claimed ignorance.

Finally, he'd been forced to pay attention to the almost obscured signs around his loading chute, the recent manure inside the narrow pathways and the tire tracks which had been nearly obliterated by the hooves of the remaining cattle. Then he had accepted the full realization that cattle thieves had been on his place and he had gone to the agency with his information.

The first possibility, they had told him, was that his cattle had been stolen by cattle thieves who had driven into his place from hundreds of miles away, those cloaked in anonymity, people whose faces he did not know. "You'd better get used to it, John B," the kid had said after he heard the facts. "Someone right around here stole them cattle. And they took them away to sell them where your brand wouldn't be known."

John's eyes left the fence lines and searched the empty sky.

from *A Yellow Raft in Blue Water*

by
Michael Dorris

Father Tom hadn't been on the reservation for two weeks before he was wearing a big beaded medallion that rode low on his black cassock. He wanted to be everybody's buddy, and thought it meant something that certain folks would smile at him out of the corner of their eyes. One time I saw him walk up, clap an old man on the back, and shout "Howdy Mr. Stiffarm, I must have missed you at church last Sunday."

Instead of answering, Grandpa Doney touched his cousin Bunky on the arm. They stood with a group passing the afternoon in front of the Agency office.

"That new priest, he's so dumb he thinks I am Henry Stiffarm," says Doney in our old-time language, raising his thin straight eyebrows and pursing his lips. "I wonder why his hair is all falling out."

"Just lucky for you he doesn't think you are *Annabelle* Stiff-arm." says Bunky, all stone-faced. "He might try to convert you then."

Annabelle is something of a legend on our reservation. Not at all hard to convert.

"I wouldn't bet on it," says Doney, rolling his eyes. That starts the whole bunch to giggling.

And Father Tom joined right in, laughing at himself like this was the funniest thing he'd ever heard. He had no idea what people thought of him. His last name was O'Connor or something, but from the first he wouldn't let anybody call him that.

"Oh no," he'd say. "Just Father Tom."

"You want to call me 'Chief Bob'?" Robert Thunderbear, our tribal chairman asked him in Indian one day, but smiled real sweet when he said it.

"Can you translate?" Father Tom whispered to Bunky, who happened to be there at the time. You could tell he was glad somebody finally said something to him.

"He said 'Welcome Young Man In Black Dress,' " said Bunky with a serious look.

Father Tom lapped that up.

I knew from the first that I would wind up Father Tom's favorite. There was no avoiding it. I was an outsider myself. All my close relatives were either dead or, like Aunt Ida who I stayed with, so old that they didn't pay me much attention. Last fall, when my mom finally died in the Seattle Indian Hospital, where she was a regular customer, the social workers shipped me back to Montana because the tribal council didn't say no. But that didn't mean they said yes either. I was on my own, and it was just a matter of time before Father Tom would discover that fact and decide I needed a role model. Him. There was no one to protect me.

Of course I didn't help matters much. Growing up in the city I never learned how to ranch but I had more school than most anyone my age on the reservation. Neither fact exactly made me fit in. And though nobody really cared who my father was, what he must have been gave some people, notably my cousins Jack and Foxy, no end of trouble.

"Hey Buffalo Soldier," they'd call to me. "When you going back to Africa?"

Even Manuel Isaacs, who had his mom's blond hair and green eyes, was no better.

"Hey Ray," he said to me one day in front of everybody, "you sure you ain't looking for the *Blackfeet* reservation? You must of took a wrong turn."

No avoiding I was going to fall into Father Tom's clutch.

I knew he'd finally heard my story the day he came up to me at Aunt Ida's and asked me to be his altar boy.

"I really need you Raymond," he said with a big wet smile. He must have counted me for at least one of those three-hundred-day indulgences each Beatitude is worth. I knew all the signs. I had been people's project before.

I admit I gave in without a fight. Father Tom was the last man on the reservation I wanted to know, but that spring he was the only one that wanted to know me. And he needed me more than he thought.

"Do you speak any of your native tongue, Raymond?" he asked me after mass the first time I served him.

Why did they always call it that?

"My Mom grew up here," I said. "She talked it at home. I can understand it okay."

"I smell like dogshit!" Father Tom boomed out at me in Indian.

I had heard him say this before. Ever since Willard Windyboy, on the council, found out that Father Tom wanted to learn the language he had been giving him special lessons.

"You shouldn't say that," I said. "Willard was pulling your leg."

Father Tom's face sagged. He looked like some kid who just dropped his popsicle in the dirt and wants to blame anybody but himself.

"What does it mean?" he demanded, but I wouldn't say.

"Just say *hello*," I told him, giving him the ordinary word, "if you have to say something."

But I could tell that *hello* didn't sound nowhere as interesting as *I smell like dogshit* to Father Tom's ear. He looked at me and didn't trust me one bit. But he had no choice.

Before too long Father Tom got to checking everything out with me before he leaped, and I got pretty well used to having him around. For one thing he never got tired of talking about sex, which he called "The Wonders of the Human Body," and that was a subject about which I had great interest but little know-how. It started one Sunday when we were walking back from the eleven o'clock mass and he asked me how old I was. I told him fourteen.

"Do you ever have *those* kind of dreams?" he asked me, blushing but trying to act like it was the most natural question in the world.

At first I thought he meant medicine dreams, which the old folks say are supposed to come around my age. The kind of dreams that tell you about who you are and what you're supposed to be. I was interested that he believed in them too.

"Not yet," I said. "But I dreamed of a bear once two years ago. Do you think that means something?"

He looked at me real strange.

"I mean dreams," he said. "About The Wonders of the Human Body."

I still looked blank.

"Sex," Father Tom said. His skin turned splotchy red and he looked like one of those mooseheads that are stuffed with a grin on their face. "Wet dreams. Do you have them?"

I was so suprised by his question that I said yes, which was a dumb thing to do because from then on he kept nagging me every chance he got to find out what I dreamed about.

"You're not supposed to tell your dreams," I told him, but he wouldn't give up.

"I can help you, Raymond," he said, again with his dead smile. "You need the guidance of an older man. You have reached the age of puberty."

Sometimes that priest made me so nervous I wanted to run from him. But there was nowhere to go. And sometimes he was all right. When I did have questions he would answer me straight out, use grown-up words, not play around and make me feel stupid.

He was always telling me to be proud of my dual heritage, as he called it. The time Foxy started going on about my Coppertone tan I was ready to pack up and hit out. Maybe I could jump the Great Northern back to Seattle and look up some of the kids I used to know. I figured I'd take off school for a day or two to plan this out, but not two hours after classes at the mission had started, who shows up at Aunt Ida's door but Father Tom.

"We missed you in religion, Raymond," he said.

"I must have slept through the alarm."

"Is something troubling you?"

It had rained the night before and the gravel in front of the house sparkled in the sunlight. The air was sharp and dry and the breeze had a bite in it. I didn't say anything, just dug the toe of my boot in the ground and waited him out.

"You know you can talk to me, Raymond," he said. He was like somebody who had just sat down to watch his favorite show on TV, like he didn't know what was going to happen next but he knew he'd enjoy it. He had on his shiny black pants and a washed-thin t-shirt, with a black windbreaker that said "Saints" on the back in gold writing. He had cut himself shaving and it looked like a vampire had dropped in on him in his sleep. His skin was so pale that the little veins showed through under his blue eyes.

"There's nothing to say," I said. "I'm just getting out of here, that's all."

He nodded, pretending to take me serious.

"And where are you off to, if I may ask?"

"Back to Seattle, maybe," I said, and then watched to see what his reaction to this idea might be. But he wasn't about to give me any clue.

"When do you leave?" he asked. He thought he was stringing me along good, just setting me up to knock my house of cards out from under me. I could smell his "counseling strategy" a mile off. This game was getting us nowhere.

"Forget it," I said. "I'll go to school. I'm not going anywhere."

Now he was disappointed. He couldn't even take credit for putting me on the right path.

"Tell you what," he said. "Come this weekend I'm borrowing Father Hurlburt's pickup and taking you up to Flathead Lake. Just us. To camp. What do you say to that?" He cracked the knuckles of his thin, white fingers hard while he was talking.

It was a time of day when nobody made noise on the reservation. People who were usually loud were either sleeping it off or sitting in school, so the quiet kind of settled down over us standing there, him waiting for me to say something and me trying to think what to say.

"I say all right," I finally said.

"*All right!*" he repeated, but a lot louder. His TV program had turned out okay after all. I'd be his sitting duck for two days.

"We'll have a chance to *talk*," he said, and reached out and shook me by the shoulder, then pulled his hand back real awkward. He was trying hard.

For the first time since I arrived back on the reservation the time passed too quickly. On Friday afternoon Father Tom, dressed in a green Sears short-sleeved western shirt and stiff new jeans pulled the mission truck up beside me as I walked on the road home from school and gave the horn three quick taps.

"All set and ready to go, Raymond!" he shouted loud enough for all the other kids to hear. "I've taken care of everything. Hop in!"

I put my head down and stepped high onto the running board, then swung myself in through the door, but not fast enough. Behind me I heard my cousin Jack say, "How many sleeping bags you bringing there, Ray-man? Two or one?"

Father Tom stopped by Aunt Ida's but she was out. I didn't have much to pack and I wanted to get away before anybody else showed up to see us leave together. It was bad enough being Father Tom's altar boy.

When I came out he was busy looking at a map he had folded up backwards. He gave off a tight, clean smell that even the open windows wouldn't let out of the cab. I noticed he had bitten his fingernails down short and square.

The truck springs were old and the road was rutted from the winter runoff, so we bounced our way to the main state highway. I didn't talk much, just answered Father Tom's questions with a word or two and kept my face in the wind, counting telephone poles. Finally, after about an hour, he snagged me.

"Tell me about your parents, Raymond. Your mother and father."

I could imagine what he'd heard.

"My Mom's dead," I said right off. No use denying that. It was a plain fact he could look up. I thought for a minute.

"My Dad's a pilot. He flies jumbos, all over the world. That's why I couldn't live with him. But he's planning to get a place, in L.A."

I never told that story before. I don't know where it came from. But I thought it wasn't bad.

"A pilot," Father Tom said, frowning his forehead and steering with one hand. "*Where* does he fly?"

"Japan. South America. Switzerland." I said, naming the first places I thought of.

Father Tom took off his sunglasses and gave me the eye like he could see whether or not I was telling the truth. But he couldn't.

"I never knew that, Raymond. I didn't know your father was living."

"Oh, he's living, all right," I said. "He's doing great."

That shut Father Tom up for a good thirty miles. We were climbing into the mountains now and it was getting dark and cold. Finally I had to roll up the window. The radio was busted, so we just sat there in the dim light of the instrument panel, waiting to get where we were going.

Father Tom could hold it no longer.

"Is there anything you want to ask me about?" he said.

I didn't say a word. The cab seemed too small a place, his words too loud. I could hear him breathing while he waited for me to answer.

"It's not easy being a boy alone at your age," Father Tom said, "when you're different."

"I'm not different."

"I mean, your dual heritage," he said. "And . . . you spend a lot of time by yourself."

"Are we going to drive all night or what?" I asked.

"Are you tired? Do you want to stop?" he wanted to know.

Suddenly that seemed even worse than to keep going, so I said no, I was fine.

"You must notice the changes in your body, the coming of your manhood," Father Tom said. Against the night sky his head looked like a comic-book drawing, round and bald on a thin neck. "Has anyone talked to you about your puberty?"

"My Dad," I said. "My Dad told me all about it. He talked about it all the time."

Father Tom was still for a minute. "I was very much like you when I was a boy," he said. "I didn't have a father either. He was killed when I was just a baby and my mother brought me up all alone. I lived with her until I went into the seminary in high school."

"I have a father," I said. Then, "Why did you go there, that seminary?"

"I always knew I had a vocation," he said. "So did my mother. Sometimes I'd try to fight it, but I always felt God's call and I had to answer."

"So you just went in?"

"I went in there for you, Raymond. I am God's helper."

Off the reservation, alone in the truck, Father Tom was different than he was back home. Here there was nobody to laugh at him. Here I was the strange one. I didn't know what to say.

"God loves you, Raymond," Father Tom said. "God is your friend."

He reached across and put his hand on top of mine where it rested on the car seat. Our hands just sat there together like that for a minute, then he squeezed my fingers and let go. I lay my head against the glass of the window and closed my eyes, trying to sleep, trying to put his words, his hand, out of my head as the springs bounced up and down and my teeth banged together in the empty night. And finally, I slept.

"Wake up, cowboy!" Father Tom said, shaking my knee.

The car was stopped at a gasoline station just outside the Flathead Lake Park entrance. It looked to be about seven A.M. and Father Tom had on his "Saints" jacket and was drinking Coke from a can.

"This is the end of the road," he said. "We're here."

He looked half-crazy, even paler than usual and his eyes all red from driving through the night. His lips were red, too, and there was a black stubble all over his cheeks.

"Do you have to take a leak?" he asked. "The can's right over there."

The gas station restroom was around the side. To get there I walked between two wrecks set up on blocks and past an overflowing trash bucket. The stale piss smell cut through the morning air, and the toilet was clogged with paper.

Back at the car Father Tom had explained to the bored, sleepy hippie pumping the gas that he was a priest, that I was really an Indian, and that we were here at the lake for some "weekend R & R." I could feel the man looking at me, searching for the Indian, and tuning out Father Tom's long string of words. I looked back at the man, stared him down, and got in. I was the only part of the story he'd remember, the only part he'd tell to other customers as the day stretched out. I'd heard people talk about me before, in Seattle.

Following the signs we came to the campsites. The park had just opened that week and so it was almost deserted, but Father Tom had to look at five or six spots before he found the one he wanted. It was some distance from the rest, behind a stand of pine, and bordered by a stream. Without talking much we set up the tent and stored the sleeping bags and food inside, then collected some wood for a fire.

"Hot dogs for lunch, Raymond," Father Tom announced. "Think you can handle four?"

The bugs were bad. Small, stinging insects that whined close to your ear and then veered away before they could be crushed. The ground was spongy and damp.

"Tell you what," Father Tom said. "Let's get out of these clothes and put on our swim suits. We'll take a dip in the lake before lunch and then have a good long talk while we eat. You've got to learn to trust me, Raymond."

There was a pier that ran for ten feet into Flathead Lake. The blue water seemed to be held in a bowl formed by the mountains that rose on every side, and it reflected the sunlight in bright planes, each dazzling as the wind stirred waves on the surface. I had never seen so much water up close. Even in Seattle we had never gone to see the Sound.

Father Tom wore red swimming trunks with a white stripe down the side. His body was hairy and soft and he wore a miraculous medal around his neck. It embarrassed me to look at him. My cutoffs, passed on to Aunt Ida for me from Foxy's mother, were too big and were held up by an elastic stretch belt. In the sunlight my skin was the color of pine sap.

Sitting on the end of the pier, Father Tom stuck his feet into the water and kicked up a spray.

"Oh Raymond," he said, laughing loudly, "it's too cold to swim. Look, I'm getting goose bumps. We'd better head back to camp."

Out about fifty feet was a wooden raft, painted yellow. Squinting past it, I could see there was someone canoeing on the far side of the lake.

"People are out there," I said. "I'm going in."

Without testing the water I ran off the end of the pier and suddenly was surrounded by pinpricks of ice, contracting my skin and blasting out the tiredness. My feet sank into plants and soft mud that squeezed between my toes as I kicked to the surface. I never knew before you could smell under the water, but I could. It smelled green and brown. I felt clean.

"Raymond," Father Tom was calling at me. He was standing with his feet apart at the end of the pier and looked upset. "You'll get a cramp. Come out."

I pretended not to hear.

"The water's fine," I shouted and started kicking and paddling away from the shore. I am no swimmer but I can stay afloat, and slowly I made progress toward the low yellow raft. By the time I got there I was out of breath and chilled. I pulled myself over the side and lay on the sun-warmed, dry boards panting and soaking up the heat. The silence was wide as the sky, brushed only with the sound of water striking the beams under the platform.

After a while I heard the splash of a dive and watched as Father Tom sidestroked his way out into the lake. He pointed his long toes with every kick, and slanted his mouth to gulp air just above the water line. He wasn't six feet from the raft when the noise suddenly stopped and he looked up at me in surprise.

"Holy Jesus," he said. "Raymond. It's too cold. I've got a cramp." Without closing his eyes his head dipped into the water as he curled into a cannonball.

"Raymond," he said, when his face rolled up again.

I jumped, the water a freezing slap against my dry skin. He had not sunk far and lay calm and pleading when I reached his side.

"Raymond," he said a third time, as I raised his chin high to the air. With my other arm grasped across his chest, I pulled him toward the worn, splintery raft. He would begin to sink whenever I let him go. He made no struggle, spoke no words. I held onto him as I threw one of my legs, then the other, onto the flat surface, then, reaching under his arms, I dragged his shoulders and chest over the edge until he could not fall back. The rough boards scraped against his skin but he made no effort to protect himself. Finally I grabbed the red trunks and hauled the rest of him out of the lake. He lay on his side, staring across the surface of the water. He started to gasp.

I was out of breath myself but I wondered about artificial respiration. I remembered something about pushing on the back and pulling on the arms. I crawled to where he lay and tried to roll him onto his stomach, but at last he resisted and instead turned to face me.

"You have saved me," he said, and reaching his arm around me he drew me close. Our chests pressed together and I could feel the pound of his heart as the medal he wore bit into me. His skin was colder than the water, his voice was hot in my ear.

"We are alone," he said, and moved to bring his body next to me. I felt him pressing, pressing, and I felt the breath leave my lungs. I wanted to sleep, to drown, to bore into the boards of the raft.

"Bless me, Father," I said in my dream.

His body stiffened. A space opened between us and I drew in air.

"Why did you say that?" Father Tom asked.

"I don't know," I said. "I guess I was afraid. I don't swim that good."

He sat up.

I rolled on my back. It was still the same day and the sky was blue.

"I'd say you swim pretty well," he said.

The skin on his stomach was red and chafed from the boards. He hugged his knees to his chest.

"What were you going to confess?" he asked, not looking at me.

"I made up all that about him being a pilot," I said. "It was a lie."

Father Tom made a sound like a crow. I couldn't tell if he was laughing or crying or clearing his throat of the last drops of swallowed water.

"I think we should go back to the reservation," he said. "I think this trip is over."

This time Father Tom had no trouble swimming. In fact, he was already half-dressed by the time I reached the pier. What little hair he had, above his ears and on the back of his head, stood out like some sort of halo from where the towel had rubbed it.

"Raymond," he said, "I should never have gone in when I was so tired. I had no rest. When we get back I think we should forget this trip ever happened. It was a bad idea. You need friends your own age. Some people might misunderstand if they see us together all the time."

He was cracking his knuckles again. The sound they made was loud and hollow like a woodpecker hammering against a dead tree.

"I'm not staying there," I told him. "I'm going to Seattle."

"Oh yes, Seattle," he said. "I'm sure you have somewhere to live in the city?"

"There are lots of places," I said. "I could look up my Dad."

"That might be just the thing for you to do," he said as if it was something funny. He nodded his head, making the halo wave like October grass in the wind.

I turned away from him and pulled my too-big pants up over my too-big wet cutoffs. He scared me the way he was acting.

"Raymond? Are you serious?"

"Yes," I said, trying to keep the fear out of my voice.

"Do you have any money?"

I didn't.

"Well, if you're truly set on going, maybe I could lend you some cash for the ticket and for cab fare from the train."

I didn't answer him.

"Are you positive that this is what you want to do?"

He was getting interested in the idea of my departure. He started skipping flat rocks across the surface of the lake while I finished dressing.

"You know," Father Tom said, "it doesn't really make a lot of sense for you to come all the way back to the reservation with me if you're going to Seattle. It's the wrong direction. I saw there's a depot right at the Park entrance."

There was no stopping him now.

"A ticket would be cheaper from here. I could put you on the train and with what you save you could take your Dad out to dinner. Then I could pick up anything you needed from your Aunt's and send it on to you."

Yesterday he hadn't believed in this Dad. Now he was buying him a meal.

"I should tell Aunt Ida," I said.

But he was ready for that too.

"I'll make a special trip up there the minute I return and explain the whole thing to her. Don't worry. I'll make sure she's all right."

I couldn't think of another reason that would get me back, so I just turned back down the trail to the campsight with my head buzzing.

We went to the next town and Father Tom called the Great Northern ticket office to find out about the train. It went through at 10:17 that night. He got me a hamburger and a sports magazine to read, and kept going on about how interesting Seattle was and what a bright young man like me could do there.

"And you won't feel so alone, so out of place," he said, smiling that stupid grin of his at me across the table. "There'll be others in the community who share your dual heritage."

The hours finally passed and we sat in the cab of the truck, waiting by the crossing for the train's beam to slice through the night. When it did, Father Tom was supposed to blink the truck headlights three times and the train would stop to pick me up. We had fallen quiet, with nothing more to say to each other.

I felt the rumble from the earth before I saw the light. First the tires, then the worn springs of the truck began to quiver and shake. Father Tom blinked the headlights once, twice, three times, and the engine began to cut down. The night was very dark.

"Raymond," said Father Tom, "I want you to have this."

He reached around his neck and pulled something over his head. I thought it was the holy medal that had cut into my chest at the lake and I reached out to take it. But instead it was the beaded medallion Father Tom wore on the reservation, big and gaudy and ugly. Tourist bait.

"Wear this," he said. "Then people will know you're an Indian."

He got out of the car with me as the train continued to slow and stuffed some dollar bills into my jeans pocket.

"Don't worry about paying me back," he said. "I know we'll meet again some day."

He grabbed me to him, quick and hard, then pushed me away just as fast.

"I'm going to leave you now, Raymond. You'll be in my prayers."

He got in the truck and backed it up to the black treeline before hitting the lights. Then he gunned the engine and turned onto the highway heading east.

He didn't look back. He didn't see me wave the train on or hear the engineer yell a fast-moving curse at goddamn Indians playing tricks. He didn't see me toss the medallion onto the track to be ground into plastic dust.

When the earth had stopped trembling, when the sounds of wind and frogs and crickets had returned, I stood still in the cold night. Clouds covered the moon and all directions were the same. I could smell the lake. I had never felt further from sleep.

I tried to remember things Mom had said about my father. There weren't enough. She only talked about him when she got mad. He'd been the best one, she'd say, because of me. Then she'd pull herself together and smile and call me her sterling silver lining.

I sat in a pocket of gravel between two ties and leaned back against the track. It was still warm from the train's passing. I was in a tight spot but it could be worse. I had the priest's money and the whole night to think before morning came. I was happy without reason.

Episodes in Mythic Verism

from *Monsignor Missalwait's Interstate*
Gerald Vizenor

Hawthorn Melody Farm Dairy . . . has begun to print photographs and descriptions of missing children on its cartons in an effort to help locate the youngsters.—*New York Times,* January 4, 1985

Listen, when milk cartons bear the pictures of stolen children then civilization needs a better trickster. Look, white people drink too much milk before they come out to play anyway.—Monsignor Missalwait

Monsignor Lusitania Missalwait was late for the last episode in his roadside war stories. Someone had locked the stout old man in an outhouse and borrowed his motorcycle; never undone, and determined to buoy his blood in white water, he pried loose the seat cover, brushed aside webs and dead flies, sloshed out the back, and marched the whole distance from the treeline to his concrete interstate in the dark.

The clerical title of honor was not an altar commission, but he does, believe it or not, own a section of interstate highway with one bridge and an exit to a small town near the White Earth Reservation where he was born on May 7, 1915, the same day the steamship *Lusitania* was torpedoed and sunk near the Irish coast. His mother was a word griever and a shaman who routed bedimmed souls and cornered wicked shadows. She held birds near her ears when she listened to men, and she healed small animals, children, and women drunkards, in that order. His father was a reservation grunter, unnamed in an oral tradition; a white woodcutter who licked a frozen bit and lost his alien tongue on the same night his last son was born and the steamer was torpedoed.

"Now, the first picture on the screen, you see, that there is where Monsignor Lusitania Missalwait was conceived," said Supine Summer, the urban war stories projectionist. Soupie, as she is known on the reservation, was the last in her families to serve tribal men and bear the names of the seasons.

The transparencies, like her surnames, dissolved on four wide screens suspended over the interstate lanes in both directions. The steamer rises, prow and funnels above the wake, and birch bark scrolls, loose plastic windows, wither in black and white. Horses hold at the pales. The peevish wind moans on the barbed wire near the shoulder.

"Shadows are thin in the cities, darker where the shamans wait," she chanted. "He brought the urban wars back home to the reservation in a sidecar, on bald tires, with this motorcycle, the one in this picture here."

Monsignor Missalwait wore a surplice on the first screen; the loose vestment dissolved and the old mixed-blood appeared in a chicken-feather headdress. On the second screen a blonde issued from the sidecar, her hair back on the wind, but she faded when a thunder cloud shrouded the pond near the mission. The third and fourth screens transmuted the faces of tribal children to wild blooms.

Summer kneaded the microphone in the narrow barter booth on the median. When she smiled her mouth turned down. The huge loudspeakers shivered and her voice boomed ten miles down the road, over the peneplain. "Watch your speed out there, and remember this, remember at the end of the week there is a celebration because my name changes with the season, and now, a march to the war stories."

Four trucks and two sedans were double-parked on the rough shoulder. Whole families watched the feral black-and-white urban battle scenes dissolve on the screens from the mound behind the barter booth. The pictures were shot low, knee high in concrete, fast foods, and broken rails. Bodies wobbled and fingers drummed in time to "The National Fencibles" and "Semper Fidelis" by John Philip Sousa. The sound track hissed, harsh snares, and a paradiddle rushed over the piccolos. Mongrels barked but their voices were lost in the march.

Minnesota, like other states on the winter rim, nurtures those wild characters who weave their blood with the seasons and who mend the seams between cold crows and withered trees, warm hands and barbed leaves, golden peaches, pinch bean schemes, and the laughter of children in the cedar. Missalwait resolved to heal ten miles of the linear world with his urban war stories. Supine holds his light and sound on the road.

The Federal Highway Commission, in accordance with federal policies to decentralize certain public services in a new spirit of capitalism, offered ten-mile sections of interstate highways for sale to the highest bidders. The new enterprise received state and federal subsidies for section maintenance, and each entrepreneur was awarded special shares in coin-operated rest-stop ventures. The new endowments, according to press releases, would encourage imaginative management practices and reduce federal costs. These ten-mile interstate endowments were made in heaven for tricksters on the move.

Monsignor Missalwait never couched an interstate interest, and he had no cash or patent land to bid; he had little more than his blood and the urban war stories he told in fair weather at a natural amphitheater behind his cabin on the reservation.

Supine Autumn, who was a bank teller at the time, told the old mixed-blood that he could bid his blood for a slice of the interstate. "The government," she said "will provide investment loans to minorities."

"Minorities?"

"Chicken feathers."

"White meat?"

"Reservation minorities," she said and then explained the provisions, prepared his application, and before her name turned to Spring he became the proud owner of ten miles of interstate.

Monsignor Missalwait wore his beaded surplice for the ownership ceremonies. Two federal officials were situated at the north end of the section. The interstate trust treaties were embossed with an oversized chop and bound with red plastic. The officials practiced their smiles, signed for the president and various government secretaries, holstered their pens, folded their ceremonial table, and turned back toward the capital.

"One buck to pass," said Missalwait.

"For what?"

"Turned the table on the great father."

"The president is not amused."

"Fine on the president."

"The president is never fined."

"The president is fined one buck to remove blankets from our reservation over this interstate which is now mine," said the old mixed-blood with his hands laced beneath the surplice. He rocked on his heels and watched the crows circle the government sedan while he explained in pious tones that his section was located on sovereign tribal land.

Spring erected barriers and then, in minutes, she unloaded two fish houses to serve as toll booths, one at each end of the interstate section. The signs explained that the ten-mile toll could be paid in cash or barter. The first receipt was issued to the president for one blanket.

Monsignor Missalwait tottered at the end of the march into the narrow barter booth. Breathless, he wiped his brow and stout neck. Summer smiled and then she pinched her nose while he explained what had happened at the outhouse. His black trousers were wet with excrement. His nostrils flared when he leaned over the microphone and concluded his series of urban war stories.

"In the beginning," he began, "we were stones that rolled down the mountains and gathered in piles here and there as we are now in cities and towns, but some stones rolled back and became tricksters."

Summer collected cash and barter from those who had arrived late to hear the stories and then she moved back from the booth, but the stench on the old mixedblood followed her in the dark. She waited in the shadows and then when he touched his ears she started the last recorded tape of his urban war stories. His voice battered the humid interstate, words mustered on precious metal, in blood, on a gold crown, on hands, ornaments:

The San Francisco Sun Dancers got hooked on their urban illusions of the past and never rolled back. Listen to their drum music, the sound is down and oppressive. Their clothes are dark, black hats, black shirts, cosmetic boots, solemn and sullen transmuted frowns. There are no trickeries in them to heal at the western drum. The beat is too dark to turn a smile in the cities. Their primal sound downs birds, hauls winter to the new gardens in the window.

Summer turned down the volume.

Indian inventions are so compelling that thousands of white people, lost and separated like their children who are pictured on milk cartons, spill out their new tribal identities each night on television talk shows, take to chicken feathers, descriptive names, and dance in isolated circles on the concrete with burnished cheeks.

Anaïs Nin wrote about the tribal inventions that wander in the cities, on a "slow walk like a somnambulist enmeshed in the past and unable to walk into the present." She saw the noble invention alone on the streets, "loaded with memories, cast down by them. . . . He saw only the madness of the world."

"Nin never owned an interstate," mocked Summer.

"She never waded through shit to quote me either," said the mixed-blood. He wrinkled his nose, removed his trousers, and pitched them over the barbed wire at the shoulder of the road.

The Indians who spurn the inventions become invisible, imperfect victims with common names. Those who boarded the colonial transition trains became proud planners and tribal merchants who shipped their new inventions back to the reservations. Nothing is secure now but silence and secrets.

Summer smirked and covered her ears.

Someone honked a horn.

Urban tribes appeared on the four screens.

Doc Cloud Burst, creator of the San Francisco Sun Dancers, keeper of urban tribal traditions, and dispenser of downtown descriptive dream names, cupped his enormous ear in the tribal manner, whipped the faces on the drum, down down down down, and wailed in cultural pain.

Cloud Burst appeared on the first screen in the back seat of a black limousine. The seats were beaded and feathers decorated the window frames. He was pictured outside various fast-food restaurants and at selected parks.

His six disciples, Bad Mouth, and her brother Knee High, Fast Food, Touch Tone, Injun Time, Fine Print, and one white skin, Token White, responded to his beck at the drum with frowns and expressions of profound cultural torment.

Urban scenes at docks and parks continued on the fourth screen, while the disciples appeared on the second and third screens over the interstate. Token White carried a bow and arrows.

"Those drum clowns live for foul weather times four," said Professor Peter Rosebed, otherwise known in more intimate circles as the Pink Stallion because he was a mixed-blood, neither red nor white. "To them humor and kindness are forms of punishment, like urban contraries, or puritanical, their fractured visions and illusions of power come from fast food, thunder, and the roar of traffic on the interstates."

"Witnesses or survivors?" the old mixed-blood mocked his own recorded voice. He leaned back, balanced in an aluminum chair behind the barter booth.

"Confessors?" asked Summer.

"You might ask if these urban tribes are witnesses or survivors? The answer is neither, there is no trace of personal experience, their lives are borrowed from the past.

"Their lives are material, the blues died on their western drums. All of them, right down to the last plastic bear claw and false braid, would rather be blonde," said the Pink Stallion. He celebrated tribal ironies, and he never missed a moment in praise of blondes.

"Darkness, total miasmal beats, for sure," he said with obvious pleasure in his choice of words. Rosebed has studied mythic structures and the oral tradition but he boasts carnal encounters rather than theoretical interruptions.

"Listen, dark skin is not the darkness."

"Nor is fair skin an illumination," said Summer. The new stories she edited, the selection of transparencies, and the events at the barter booth, were more interesting than her studies at college and her duties at the bank. "These three-part voice dramas are the best, and you even pay me more than the bankers."

"These poor urban savages are the perfect hosts for failure and cultural contradictions," announced Monsignor Missalwait. The loudspeakers hissed and then clicked several times. The mixed-blood had tapped the microphone with his ring during the recording.

Rosebed was standing under the sycamores when a tall blonde, known as the nude dance advocate, danced like a sunbeam over the dark thunder at the western drum, and as she danced she removed her blouse and flashed her small firm white breasts.

"What the hell are you doing in there?" a woman asked. Her voiced boomed over the loudspeakers, repeated the question, and then an engine roared. Missalwait had forgotten to stop the tape recorder when her car approached the barrier and now the conversation from the barter booth was broadcast as part of the urban war stories.

"One dollar," answered Monsignor Missalwait.

"Don't have a dollar."

"What do you have?"

"Nothing," said the woman.

"Come to the stories then," he said.

"What stories?"

"Free urban war stories."

"When?"

"Sunday night with pictures."

"God willing," she said with a salute and roared past the booth when he raised the barrier. She honked and blinked the lights when she heard the recorded conversation that night.

Cloud Burst whipped the faces on the dream drum harder, thundered hard, and raised his voice to a pitched pain. Small leaves trembled on the trees. Between wails, he motioned with his thin lips, in the tribal manner, toward his disciples. Token White nodded back from the drum circle. She protected her drum father and moved toward the blonde with the little breasts.

Token White, tall, thin, angular, with an unattractive gait and downward curl to her lower lip, was the one blonde member of the San Francisco Sun Dancers. She danced for father sun, her special burden, and bore his dream name. Born on a corn farm she came to urban studies on a scholarship but double-crossed the academic world with terminal creeds.

White became a master archer, an expert on bows and arrows, and turned tribal in place of books and theories. She embodied total racial, spiritual, and cultural opposition behind the bow; an archer at war with civilization and technologies. White hates her color and shape in the world, and she shares this hatred with the urban tribes who hate whites.

Token White lumbered over to the nude dance advocate and drew her bow with a black arrow. She followed the blonde as she rolled her shoulders and breasts in sensual semicircles. The drum thundered at the side.

"Classic, this is a classic scene," raved the Pink Stallion in the thunder and sunshine. "This is the perfect demonstration of double cultural contradictions. Those two should cancel each other out, like double negatives. Two blondes, one a token in opposition to the other with the same reasons."

"What was that?" asked Summer.

"Blondes are in perfect opposition to the invented tribes, but pardon me for loving blondes, and nude dance advocates, more than throwback archers in black hats."

"Do you know this person?" asked Summer.

"Too much oral tradition," answered Missalwait.

"Behind the counter."

"Token White uses tribal culture like a prescription for a headache," said Rosebed, "look at her there, built like a crooked limb, crude like a bad bow, while the blonde dancer moves through culture from the inside, her side, our side, not the outside, not a deprivation model for culture, not a mere concept for being alive, she is alive.

"The urban tribes have it all turned around, too much tradition on the mind and not enough heart in the crotch," Rosebed said with his hands on his crotch. "Prescription cultures bind them in time, too much owned from the past tenses, dreams and the inside are closed down for repairs, not enough celebration of light and real flesh.

"Listen, blondes are wonderful, but tribal culture and blondes are like bad doctors for the soul," he said and his wild hands cut each word to size.

"Listen, white bitch, our dream drum music is sacred," snapped Token White to the blonde dancer who cupped her breasts and shimmered once more over the thunder and through the pain.

"Monsignor Lusitania Missalwait, is that the name of a real priest?" asked a man at the barrier. He leaned out the window closer to the barter booth to hear, unaware that his voice was recorded with the last episode of the urban war stories.

"That is my whole name," said the mixed-blood.

"The province or the liner?"

"What does he mean by that?" asked Summer.

"The liner," he told the man at the barrier.

"Portugal was once named Lusitania," he explained to Summer.

"Why not the nation then?" she asked.

"Named for the dead?" asked the recorded voice.

"Mother Missalwait was a griever," said the old mixed-blood. "She set the world right with words, like a table, but it was never the same from meal to meal, tree to tree, season to season, because she believed that what ended by chance was never dead, but waited for a time to be discovered in dreams and names. So, the steamer returned with me one night, nine months from a wild conception over wild rice in a rented canoe.

"When were you ordained?"

"Let me answer that," she said. Summer leaped from her aluminum chair and waded like a heron around the barter booth. "The mission priest said he was real touched, he said he could patch leaks better than any half-breed he ever knew on the reservation, but that was nothing to remember when he started his stories about the urban tribes in the cedar theater out back.

"August 12, 1970."

"Lusitania heals birds like his mother, but he never did like drunkards," Summer continued between recorded voices. The transparencies dissolved with the conversations and somehow the narrative made sense because more than a dozen families stopped on the shoulder to watch and listen. "Then we discovered that when he was at the natural theater behind his cabin there were no flies or mosquitoes there, and when the thunder boomed all around it never rained when he was there. He was ordained by nature, in the cedar, and all the mixed-bloods agreed."

"Dominus vobiscum," chanted Missalwait.

"Would you like to sell your interstate?" the man asked.

"Never."

"Never, is right," said Summer.

"Does it rain here?" asked the recorded voice.

"Not on the barter booth."

"But tell me, are you a real Indian?"

"Partial invention."

"This is an honoring song, bitch," Token White hissed through her clenched teeth. "No bare tits allowed, so move out before we honor your ass with an arrow."

Cloud Burst waited for her to return during the last night of her urban vision search. The other members of the San Francisco Sun Dance all started for their four-night vision in the same urban place and returned on time to meet father sun in the morning.

Token White started at Union Square with no money, no food, and the same instructions as the others to seek an urban vision on the streets. She was the first white skin to be initiated and now she was late for her dream-name ceremonial.

Each disciple received the same sacred instructions to return to the old traditions in mind and heart, speak to the four directions and to four people on the streets: an old man who remembers the past, mother earth, and her two children the sun and water spirits. The visioneers were told to live on the streets, in dumpsters but not hotel lobbies, for four nights in search of a personal spiritual guardian and then to walk across the Golden Gate Bridge to the ceremonial bunker at Fort Cronkite, near Rodeo Lagoon.

The disciples were pierced on the breasts with plastic skewers fastened to leather laces bound to the sacred cottonwood tree at the ceremonial bunker. The disciples faced the rising sun, their father, and danced in circles on mother earth until a dream name was called out for the first time.

Cloud Burst told his sacred dancers that he learned in a dream that Token White would be late. He had a similar dream when Injun Time was late, but because it rained that morning, father sun was also late so Fine Print saved the day when he raised a new father sun made from orange aluminum foil on a broom handle. Since then, and because the weather is seldom clear in the morning over the ceremonial bunker, the San Francisco Sun Dancers raise and lower their own sun in their own sacred time.

Token White drew her Navajo bow three hours before dawn on the fourth night and threw four flaming reed arrows over the ceremonial bunker from the four directions. The sinew hummed with each arrow.

Cloud Burst said the flaming arrows were all according to his dream. The disciples saw the arrows as a sacred message from the great spirit. Then Token White threw a padded arrow into the bunker with a note attached. A message was printed on plain brown paper. Cloud Burst, who could not read, passed the note to Fine

Print who cleared his throat and then imitated the halting voice of his spiritual leader as he read:

Father Cloud Burst
you sure did trust me to be a disciple
and my heart pounded like a medicine drum
But because my skin is white
my shadow is white too
which makes me feel ashamed father
I am over the hill now
but if you want me call me from the four directions
and I will come to be pierced
and never return to my white shadow again

Fine Print cleared his throat at the end of the message. The ceremonial bunker was silent. Ocean waves lapped over the rocks on the shore. The air was moist and cold, too cold to bare a chest. The disciples waited for their leader to instruct them.

Cloud Burst motioned with his hands and head in the four directions, to the stars and the moon, rubbed his face and bare chest with smoke from the cedar fire, and then he began to wail in a low voice. He wailed until he slipped through his own shadow in a vision and then he pierced his chest muscles with plastic skewers once more, in the same old scars, for the sacred sun dance. He leaned back, danced in a slow circle, and pulled the leather laces tight from the cottonwood tree in the center of the bunker. Fine Print danced on the other side of the tree with his father.

Cloud Burst wailed and Fine Print wailed and the two danced in circles on mother earth, the new concrete mother earth, for more than an hour and then the two stopped. The bunker was silent again. The ocean wind howled in the weeds. The fire snapped. Birds loomed from the ocean.

Cloud Burst raised his arms, pulled back hard on the leather laces until his flesh ripped open, the cottonwood tree shuddered in place, and he called her dream name for the first time in the four sacred directions.

"Token White," he called to the north.

"Token White," Summer called to the west.

"Token White," he called to the south.

"Token White," the families on the shoulder called to the east. Horns honked and lights blinked in celebration. The disciples appeared on the four screens, poised around a cedar fire like lost animals.

"Token White, come home to your father, come home now, come home, give yourself to father sun, come home to the bunker and be a proud urban tribal warrior with white skin." The voice of the urban sun dancer boomed in the darkness.

"Come home to the barter booth," mocked Summer.

"Here I come," said Token White with tears bouncing down her low angular cheek bones. She lumbered over the hill through the succulent plants with her bow and arrows, the new urban warrior from the invented past.

Cloud Burst, her new father with the sun, took her in his arms near the cottonwood tree. The warm blood on his chest spread on her breasts. He moved back and opened her flannel shirt near the fire. Steam rose from her dark wide nipples. He pierced her hard breasts with the same plastic skewers that cut his flesh, for the ceremonial erection of her new father sun.

Token White danced in hundreds of circles, tireless, each new move a wonderful dream world, around and around the cottonwood tree, she would not break. Fine Print tired, the foil sun on the pole leaned low on the bunker horizon. Cloud Burst put his arms around her from behind, cupped her breasts, and then leaned backwards with her and pulled the skewers from her little breasts. He turned her around and while she wailed he sucked the blood from her nipples and then spread her warm blood on his forehead and cheeks. The other disciples copied their master.

"Urban savages," someone called from the darkness when the four screens pictured her breasts and the cheeks of the disciples covered with blood.

"We want our money back."

"But the war stories are free."

"Never mind," said Summer.

Token White braced her short curved Apache bow, made from

a white hickory wheel hoop, drew a hazel-wood arrow with trimmed woodpecker feathers and a hand-flaked obsidian point, the one she learned how to make in the mountains, and aimed it at the bare-breasted blonde dancer.

The dancer faced the sun at noon. She rolled her head and shoulders several times before she noticed the archer crouched behind the pruned trees at the rim of the campus plaza. She rolled to the sun once more, shivered in the face of violence, and then covered her breasts and moved into the crowd. The blonde smiled from a distance and became a passive white witness to tribal events.

"Shit, man, these white blondes are sick, sick, sick, sick," Bad Mouth screamed from the pruned sycamores. Knee High repeated each of her words, a whispered echo like a puppet at her side.

"First the blondes are boiled in hate, then comes cultural genocide, academic white tape, and then she bedews colonialism with her extreme spittle," said Rosebed, "Bad Mouth has a terminal case of colonial throat."

"Colonial throat?" asked Summer.

"The real colonist is a crazed blonde caught at the back of her throat," said Rosebed. His laughter was too loud to share the humor of the obscene gestures that followed his description.

"Deep throat," someone chanted from the shoulder.

"Never mind," said Summer. She rushed to the barter booth and turned the volume higher on the recorder to override the voices of the chanters in the trucks near the second screen.

White lowered her bow and returned the arrow to her beaded whole otter-skin quiver. She sat in the sacred circle of thunder at the western drum.

"More tits and less drums," a voice demanded.

"No drums," said Summer.

White confessed her discoveries of tribal people at a summer seminar on child development. When she was thirteen, tall and unattractive for her age, she said, she discovered Indians in the book *Ishi in Two Worlds,* by Theodora Kroeber. White told how Ishi became her best friend for at least two years, until Doc Cloud Burst called her dream name in the four directions at the bunker.

Ishi taught her how to use a bow and arrow to hunt food in the wooded mountains near Mount Lassen. White said she was caught with Ishi, the last two survivors of the Yahi tribe; she confessed that she was taken with Ishi to live in the Museum of Anthropology at the University of California.

"It was in the late summer," she told the students that summer, "in the morning, near a slaughter house, when the two of us were cornered by dogs against a corral fence. We were brave, and I told Ishi the things the sheriff said when we were locked up in cells because he could not speak our language. We were tired and hungry. Then all sorts of skins came to our cell, talking in all different languages, and we understood what the skins said but we did not answer because the whites were listening.

"The sheriff showed us the headlines about us in the newspapers. We were wild Indians, and I was embarrassed, but the stories helped us to meet some good white people. We got to know some very important anthropologists, everyone should know at least one anthropologist, and we liked them too, Alfred Kroeber and Thomas Waterman, and then there was a medical doctor, Saxton Pope, he was an archer and we liked him the best.

"Ishi and Doctor Pope taught me all that I know about bows and arrows and hunting. Well," she said and looked past Sather Tower to Strawberry Creek Canyon, "we hated crowds, and when the museum opened, Phoebe Apperson Hearst, and Benjamin Ide Wheeler, he was the president of the University of California then, and other important people came to look at us in the museum like we were freaks or something in a circus.

"It hurts me now to tell you this," said White. "Ishi started to cough in the museum, he seemed tired, he had gained too much weight, we both did when we were captured, and he died in the spring. Doctor Pope was there. Ishi smiled at both of us before he started walking backwards into the next world.

"I ne ma yahi . . . wahle injin, Ishi said, which meant, *are you an indian . . . valley indian,"* said Token White. "He also said *kopee* for *coffee* and I loved him more than anyone else in the whole wide world," she said, tears down her cheeks, "until I met Doc Cloud Burst, now he is my father. When Ishi died I turned

back to the mountains to be alone and wild, and it was there that
I learned more about bows and arrows."

Pink Stallion asked her what she did in the mountains and
she said that she had been an eagle and a bear and an otter, in
that order, and once "I was even a mountain stream running down
through the redwoods to the sea."

"You dumped that to dance around a western drum?" asked
Rosebed with one finger on his nose. She was nervous from the
dance and her dense armpits had an acrid odor.

"Streams were not enough," answered White.

"Neither are bears," said Summer.

"Show me your bows," said the Pink Stallion.

"Not a chance," answered Summer.

"Do you know about bows?" she asked and handed him several. Rosebed touched the wood and strummed the sinew. She
told him how to throw an arrow and how to make points from
obsidian. When she spoke she drew civilization into the wilder-
ness, into the mountains and down the streams in her imagination and memories.

The first bow was a short bow, her "sacred bow," she said, a
Yahi bow, "the bow Ishi taught me to make from a single piece of
mountain juniper." She braced the bow and pointed out the natural deer sinew string and the graceful oval curve of the limbs.
The string snapped and hummed with a "sweet tune," she said,
and explained what she meant.

"Sweet must be sweet," mocked the Pink Stallion.

"Sweet to the archer means well balanced," she said and then
explained that the arrows were made from hazel sticks and rolled
over heated stones to make them smooth. "Ishi taught me how to
make smooth arrows."

The arrows had four feathers, trimmed feathers for a better
spin in flight. White pointed out that "Ishi used three feathers,
one bird wing for each arrow."

Doctor Saxton Pope taught her how to make the other bows.
She told two more stories, however, before she presented the other
bows. One was about riding on horseback with Doctor Pope and

Ishi back to the mountains to live in the old way. "Ishi called animals in the sacred manner of a hunter, he had a sweet voice."

The second event she told about was the time she went swimming in the nude in Deer Creek with Ishi and Doctor Pope and his son. White was embarrassed when she told these stories, she seemed concerned what people might think.

She told stories from visual memories, from the oral tradition, she was there in the places she described. Rosebed pretended to be there, he smiled when he saw her in the nude. She was embarrassed for her wide nipples and the angular shape of her body.

"More, more, more than blood," several voices chanted when she appeared on the first and second screens. The transparencies dissolved when she turned toward the camera.

The Mohave bow, she told the Pink Stallion, is made from a single stave of willow, smoked in cedar to temper the wood. The bark from the limb was still on the back of the bow. Holding the bow she explained that "this bow is better in the morning when it is cool, because the wood is harsh in warm temperatures."

"Me bones too," said Summer.

"This is my sweetest bow, it hums with a fine balance," said White. The Navaho bow was made from mesquite wood with a buckskin bound handgrip. White used the Navaho bow to throw four flaming arrows over the ceremonial bunker.

The last bow in her collection was the Apache bow, the one made from a white hickory wagon hoop which she used to draw an arrow on the nude dancer. "This is my cupid bow, because it has a wheel curve to the limbs."

Pink Stallion stroked the curve and snickered.

Cloud Burst reset his black wide brimmed hat, whipped the same old faces on the drum one last time, and ended the honoring music for students on campus. The other drummers knew when to stop; they raised their wands like shorebirds, beaks high near the ocean waves, and the beat ended. The urban tribes drum and summon the thunder to know the silence.

"So ends the first series of urban war stories," said Monsignor Missalwait. His motorcycle was the last picture to dissolve on the four screens over the interstate. He thought he heard the engine in the distance.

"Autumn is my birthday next week," said Summer.

"Remember Soupie."

"No tolls on my birthday."

"Listen, whoever borrowed my motorcycle would you please return it now," the mixed-blood pleaded over the loudspeakers. "We might have to run curious blondes to the cedar theater for a screen test, mea culpa, mea culpa."

Sam English, *Tribute to Himself.* Oil, mixed media, 36 by 48 inches.

Contributors

Louise Erdrich is the author of *Jacklight,* a book of poems, and *Love Medicine,* a novel, for which she received the 1984 National Book Critics Circle Award. Erdrich is a member of the Turtle Mountain Band of Chippewa and grew up in Wahpeton, North Dakota. She is a graduate of Dartmouth College, where she participated in the Native American Program, and of the Writing Program at Johns Hopkins University. Currently she lives in New Hampshire with her husband, Michael Dorris, and their children. *The Beet Queen,* Erdrich's second novel, from which "The Manifestation at Argus," included here is taken, will be published in early 1986.

A member of the Osage tribe, **Glen Martin** is a freelance writer born in Utah and currently living in northern California. His articles have appeared in a very large number of magazines and newspapers, including *Audubon, Outside, Sports Afield, Outdoor Life,* and the *San Francisco Examiner.* In addition to nonfiction, Martin also writes and publishes both poetry and fiction.

One of the most widely published of American Indian writers, **Linda Hogan** is a member of the Chickasaw tribe and currently part of the American Studies faculty at the University of Minnesota. Her poems have appeared in three collections—*Calling Myself Home, Daughters, I Love You,* and *Eclipse*—and her poetry and short fiction have appeared in dozens of magazines and journals such as *Prairie Schooner, Denver Quarterly,* and *Greenfield Review.* In addition, her writing has been included in more than fifteen anthologies.

N. Scott Momaday, Kiowa and Cherokee, was born in Lawton, Oklahoma, and spent most of his youth in the Southwest. He has B.A., M.A., and Ph.D. degrees and has taught at such universities as the University of California at Santa Barbara, the University of California at Berkeley, Stanford University, and the University of Arizona, where he is currently professor of English. Momaday has received numerous awards, including a John Jay Whitney Foundation Fellowship, a Guggenheim Fellowship, and a Fulbright Fellowship. In 1969 he received a Pulitzer Prize for his first novel, *House Made of Dawn.* His publications include *Angle of Geese and Other Poems, The Journey of Tai-Me, The Way to Rainy Mountain, The Gourd Dancer, The Names: A Memoir,* and poems, stories, and essays in many journals and anthologies.

Paula Gunn Allen describes herself as Laguna/Sioux/Lebanese-American. Born in Albuquerque and raised in Cubero, New Mexico, she holds B.A., M.F.A. and Ph.D. degrees and has taught at several universities. Allen's many awards include an NEA Fellowship for Writing, a Post-Doctoral Fellowship in American Indian Studies (UCLA), a Research Grant from the Ford Foundation and National Research Council Fellowship, and an appointment as Associate Fellow at Stanford Humanities Institute. Her publications include *The Woman Who Owned the Shadows,* a novel (1983), as well as numerous collections of poetry and essays. Her poetry, short fiction, and essays have appeared in many journals and anthologies, and her collection of essays, *The Sacred Hoop: Essays on American Indian Life and Thought,* will be published by Beacon Press in early 1986.

Louis Owens, Choctaw, Cherokee, and Irish-American, grew up in Mississippi and California. He holds B.A., M.A., and Ph.D. degrees from the University of California and has taught at the University of California, Davis, the University of Pisa (on a Fulbright Fellowship), California State University, Northridge, and the University of New Mexico, where he is currently an assistant professor. Owens has published two book-length critical studies as well as short fiction, essays, and nonfiction articles in numerous magazines and journals.

Elizabeth Cook-Lynn currently teaches at Eastern Washington State University, Cheney, Washington, where she is associate professor of English and Indian Studies. She is a member of the Crow Creek Sioux tribe and received her education at South Dakota State University and the University of South Dakota as well as the University of Nebraska and Stanford University. Elizabeth Cook-Lynn's writing has appeared in numerous journals and anthologies, including *Prairie Schooner* and *Sun Tracks.*

Michael Dorris, a member of the Modoc tribe, grew up in Washington, Idaho, Kentucky, and Montana. After receiving degrees in English from Georgetown University and in anthropology from Yale, he founded the Native American Studies Program at Dartmouth College, where he is now a full professor. Dorris is co-author of *A Guide to Research on North American Indians* and has published in a large number of magazines and journals. He has recently received the Indian Achievement Award from the Chicago Indian Council Fire and was awarded a Rockefeller grant to study the effects on certain American Indian communities of an increasing portion of babies born with fetal alcohol syndrome. Dorris is married to poet and novelist Louise Erdrich.

Gerald Vizenor, a Chippewa enrolled at the White Earth Reservation in Minnesota, was born in Minnesota. He served with the U.S. Army in Japan and after his discharge studied at New York University and received a B.A. degree from the University of Minnesota. Vizenor has been director of Inter-Cultural Programs at Park Rapids, Minnesota, and has served as director of the American Indian Employment and Guidance Center in Minneapolis. In addition, he has been Director of American Indian Studies at both Bemidji State College in Minnesota and the University of California, Berkeley, where he currently teaches. Vizenor's many publications include a novel, *Darkness in Saint Louis Bearheart* (1978) and more than a dozen collections of poems, translations, and essays.

Sam English, whose paintings appear on the jacket of this book and on page 128, is a Chippewa artist represented by the Native American Art Gallery, 2113 Charlevoix NW, Albuquerque, New Mexico 87104.